*Fylling's Illustr*

# PACIFIC COAST TIDE POOLS

Marni Fylling

*Foreword by Chris Giorni*

H
Heyday, Berkeley, California

The publisher wishes to thank the Moore Family Foundation
and Tree Frog Treks for their generous support of this project.

*Library of Congress Cataloging-in-Publication Data*
Fylling, Marni.
Fylling's illustrated guide to Pacific coast tide pools / Marni Fylling ; foreword by Chris Giorni.
pages cm
Includes bibliographical references.
ISBN 978-1-59714-302-8 (pbk.)
1. Tide pool ecology--Pacific Coast (U.S.) 2. Tide pool animals--Pacific Coast (U.S.) 3. Tide pools--Pacific Coast (U.S.) 4. Marine ecology--Pacific Coast (U.S.) 5. Marine animals--Pacific Coast (U.S.) I. Title. II. Title: Illustrated guide to Pacific coast tide pools.
QH541.5.S35F95 2015
577.690979--dc23

2014041186

Cover Art: Giant Pacific Octopus, *Enteroctopus dofleini*
Cover Design: Ashley Ingram
Interior Design/Typesetting: Rebecca LeGates

Published by Heyday
P.O. Box 9145, Berkeley, California 94709
(510) 549-3564
heydaybooks.com

Printed in East Peoria, Illinois, by Versa Press, Inc.

10 9 8

# CONTENTS

"It is advisable to look from the tide pool to the stars
and then back to the tide pool again."

—John Steinbeck, *The Log from the Sea of Cortez*

*For Mom, Dad, and Rowan, with love*

# ACKNOWLEDGMENTS

CHRIS GIORNI IS THE REASON you're holding this book in your hands. We met many years ago at the Bodega Marine Lab, where I saw my first tide pools. Thank you, Chris, for giving me the idea for this guide, along with your unbridled enthusiasm and support. Lucky me.

The cheerful, committed crew at Heyday made this process a pleasure—thank you, Lillian, Ashley, Mariko, and Rebecca, and special thanks to Gayle, Jeannine, and Diane.

I have been fortunate to have so many wonderful teachers, a loving family, and special friends who are still helping me discover and navigate the world around me. Mom and Hal, and Dad and Marilyn, got me off to a good start; Mick and Rowan are my fans at home. (Mick broke his scanner, scanning all these illustrations!) Thank you.

And for everybody to whom I've jokingly offered cookie recipes and marine invertebrate identification in exchange for their brilliant technological/dental/medical/legal assistance—here's that second part. Call me for recipes. Thank you!

# FOREWORD

# *Time to Tide Pool*

Everything flows to the sea—let's go, too, you and me, on a blue-green adventure to the beautiful and bizarre world of the tide pools. Look up and around. It's time to "re-wild yourself," as the artist Asher Jay says. It's time to scan the horizon for brown pelicans gliding effortlessly over the curving waves, to smell the sweet salt air and spy lined shore crabs scuttling about over the algae-covered rocks.

Check your tide tables, put away your cell phone, and listen to the crash of the waves. Feel the sand beneath your feet and the ocean mist on your face. Feel the calmness that comes with wide-open horizons. Refresh and recharge as you re-nature your life. Watch the rocks getting slapped by the swirling surf, covered in sea-foam one moment and revealing bright orange and purple sea stars the next. A hermit crab races by. A sea anemone dances with the waves. Pink coralline algae paints the rocks, and alien-looking sea slugs swim upside down. Tide pool sculpins flash by, masters of speed and camouflage. All of these creatures have evolved crafty strategies to withstand this harsh environment of battering waves and periodic drought.

Ever wonder what that squishy creature covered with little rocks and pebbles is, over by the edge of the shore? When the tide comes in, it blossoms into a small flower with red-tipped petals. Marni Fylling's illustrated guide will let you know that you've found a group of aggregating sea anemones. Read on and you will learn more about their behavior. Each group has its own unique colony, and they may wage minibattles with the neighboring colonies, reaching over to sting them with half-inch-long tentacles armed with microscopic venomous harpoons.

When I first met Marni, over twenty-seven years ago at a class on Bodega Bay marine invertebrate zoology offered by UC Berkeley, she amazed me with her drawings of itty-bitty squid larvae. As you thumb through this field guide, you will see that her drawings explode off the page into life. No matter who you are or what you do, this book is for you. It will enrich your experience and introduce you to the giant green anemone, the purple shore crab, and other small but wondrous creatures. A new friendship awaits when you learn a name—for example, Toni, or *Tonicella lineata,* the beautifully colored lined chiton that looks like a hand-painted Tuscan ceramic. He waits for you in plain view, fastened to an outcrop. Soon the tide pools will get under your skin and all your salty dawg seafaring friends will be calling you back again and again. These are friendships that will last a lifetime. As Rachel Carson said in her seminal book *Silent Spring,* "Those who contemplate the beauty of the Earth find reserves of strength that will endure as long as life lasts." There is no better way to connect to nature than to go tide pooling.

Once I took a group of city kids tide pooling at Duxbury Reef near Bolinas. Many of them had never been to the ocean before and did not even want to set foot off the bus for fear of getting their new shoes dirty. They all stood by the edge of the trail staring out at the sea. I stepped into a small pool, displayed my dripping shoe, and beckoned. "It is okay to get wet—come on, let's go on an adventure!" Soon all of them were marveling at black turban snails and hermit crabs. By the end of the day they were completely in the moment, acting like seals on the beach, lying on their bellies, calling out "Ark, Bark, Lark!" as the tide rolled in and covered them with sand and water. There was much excited chatter on the bus ride home that day.

Who knows? Maybe one day a child's tide pooling experience will inspire a new and efficient way to harness the great energy of the tides and power a new generation of inventors and innovators. Biomimetics strives to mimic nature's solutions. For example, mussels secrete a substance—byssal threads—to help secure them to the wet, cold, salty rocks. How do they do it? We don't know! But if we did, scientists speculate, it would be really helpful in repairing bones and tendons. After all, contact lenses were invented by studying the clear scale covering the eyes of snakes and some geckos. Get ready for gecko-inspired sticky-toe-pad tape! Sharkskin is covered in little skin teeth called dermal denticles that channel water and repel algae and barnacles. This has inspired fast swimsuits and a special coating for hospital surfaces to resist bacterial growth. Studying termite dens led to more efficient office buildings, burrs led to velcro, whale fins to super-efficient turbines, and avian migrations to jet plane formations that save fuel.

It may take some planning and even a little coaxing to get out of the house (especially if, like me, you have three kids!) but you will never regret it. Bring an extra pair of shoes and socks just in case. Whenever I go tide pooling I make it a point to walk straight into the water because once you're wet, you're wet: then you can dive right in and let the adventure begin. Lace up your old sneakers, and let's get out and get dirty. Build a fort, climb a tree, hold a bug, smell the sea!

Chris Giorni
*Director and Head Frog, Tree Frog Treks*

# INTRODUCTION

THE ROCKY SHORES OF THE Pacific coast are home to some of the world's most astonishingly diverse and spectacular intertidal life-forms. When the tide goes out, a vibrant world is revealed, and in tide pools—the pools of water left behind among the rocks—you will find the kinds of creatures otherwise seen only by divers and aquarium visitors: giant green anemones, orange and purple sea stars, red sponges, scurrying hermit crabs, and many more.

The area in which tide pools occur is called "intertidal" because it is between the tides: underwater at high tide and above water at low tide. Most of the creatures that live here are invertebrates (without backbones), most of the "plants" are algae, and all have remarkable adaptations that enable them to survive in a harsh habitat where they are completely submerged, left high and dry in the sea air, pounded by rough surf, and tormented by extreme fluctuations in temperature and salinity (saltiness).

Despite these dangers, every inch of the intertidal zone teems with life, and for good reason. These shores possess a unique combination of conditions: mild winters make freezing and being scraped by ice unlikely; summer fog mitigates heat and dryness; the varied substrate provides lots of places to cling to and hide in; and the constant wave action brings with it a life-sustaining mix of oxygen, minerals, microscopic plankton, and organic debris (bits of dead algae and animals, and animal waste).

## TIDES AND ZONES

Along the Pacific coast there are two low tides (one lower than the other) and two high tides (also of different height) almost every day. It's the dynamic nature of these changing tides that makes intertidal life so wonderfully complex here. A couple square inches of rock may house members of ten or more major phyla: perhaps worms, sponges, mollusks, arthropods, marine algae, echinoderms, flatworms, bryozoans, tunicates, and fishes. And very few of them can live anywhere else. The extreme nature of the environment, caused by conditions that—with the tides—are rapidly and constantly changing, requires extremely specialized adaptations.

Tides are caused by the gravitational attraction between the earth, the moon, and the sun. The gravitational pull of the moon pulls the earth and the earth's water toward the moon,

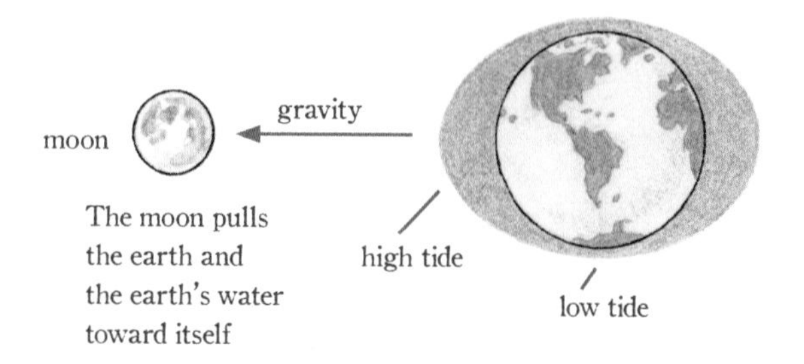


*Tidal activity is largely due to the moon's gravitational pull. Local wind and weather patterns can also affect the tides.*

SPLASH ZONE
Tide pool life occurs at different levels, or "zones."
HIGH TIDE LINE
MIDDLE INTERTIDAL ZONE
LOW TIDE LINE

and the sun also affects the tides, but to a lesser extent because of its distance from the earth. The rotation of the earth and the position of the moon in its orbit lead to variations in high and low tides, with the extremes occurring when the moon is full or new.

Tide pool animals and algae occur at different levels, ranging from the heights of the "splash zone" to the low intertidal, and down to the subtidal zone.

The top level, the *splash zone,* is at the highest reach of ocean spray and storm waves, and it is never submerged.

The *high intertidal* zone is under water only during the highest high tides. Animals and algae here are used to being out of the water more than they are in it.

The *mid-intertidal* zone includes the "zero" on tide tables—the level from which plus and minus tides are measured—and is flooded about twice every day.

The *low intertidal* zone is submerged most of the time: it's only revealed during minus tides, for a few hours each month.

The *subtidal* zone is under water at all but extreme low tides. Creatures living here have a very low tolerance for heat or desiccation (drying out).

Among these zones, the upper limit of a species depends upon how much exposure to air and sun it can withstand. The lowest level is determined by an organism's ability to compete with other species and avoid predation; where there is abundant moisture, there is plenty of competition.

Tide pools offer a bit of a respite from some of the dangers of the intertidal zone: the trapped water allows animals and algae to enjoy some of the benefits of lower tide levels while being higher up than many of their predators. In fact, tide pools function as nurseries for any number of invertebrates and ocean-going fishes. They are a safe(ish) place in which to grow large enough to survive in the outside world.

The "safety" of tide pools comes with challenges. The temperature and salinity of the ocean are fairly stable: most sea creatures can't survive outside this narrow range. As the sun beats down on a tide pool, the water loses much of its oxygen—and it's just hot! And as the water evaporates, the salinity shoots up. And conversely, if it rains, the seawater is diluted to dangerously low salinity.

As you explore the tide pools, notice how different animals use their bodies or behavior to protect themselves from drying out, washing away with the waves, or being eaten by predators. Tough skins, thick shells, and sliminess are good for keeping moist, as are behavioral adaptations like clustering together, hiding under cool clumps of algae, or crawling into wet crevices. Many of these features are also useful to avoid becoming a predator's dinner, as are camouflage and fighting back with spines, claws, stingers, or nasty chemicals.

## LIFE ATTACHED TO THE ROCKS

Animals and algae that permanently attach to the rocks (or each other!) must have special ways to find food, reproduce, and get their young out into the world. Sponges and tunicates use their bodies to create a water flow that brings food to them; many filter feeders use legs or tentacles to strain the water or search their surroundings for tasty bits.

Finding a mate is also a problem for the permanently attached. Quite a few members of the intertidal zone reproduce by flinging tremendous numbers (hundreds to thousands) of sperm and eggs out into the ocean (much as trees send their pollen out on the wind) in hopes that these gametes will find each other. The results of such unions are tiny swimming larvae, microscopic critters that look nothing like their parents. Like dandelion seeds flying off in all directions—and unlike their sedentary parents—the young can move to new locations, and since they don't settle next to their parents, they don't compete with them for precious food or space. Alas, most of the larvae become dinner for any number of fishes or invertebrates; they are an important part of the ocean's food web. The few that survive find a nice place to call home, settle, and metamorphose into adults.

It takes a lot of energy to produce eggs or sperm in quantities that will insure the survival of a few new animals. So when conditions are favorable, intertidal creatures such as anemones, sponges, and tunicates quickly add to their ranks by asexual reproduction, forming clones of themselves. They don't get the benefit of genetic diversity or dispersal to new environs, but it's an easy way to spread over an area without the high cost of sexual reproduction.

## A NOTE ABOUT BINOMIALS

The common names used for the algae and animals in this book are convenient to use in casual conversation, but they are like nicknames, with some of the same liabilities. The same animal may have multiple common names: the "red rock crab" may be called a "red crab" or a "red cancer crab," depending on what region the speaker is from, or just what he or she is used to. To add to the confusion, one common name may be used for different species—at least three different kinds of crabs in the world are all called "red rock crabs."

The scientific names found alongside the illustrations in this book (and in the appendix) are specific to each creature.

A scientific name, or "binomial," has two parts, the genus and species, usually from Greek or Latin. The red rock crab in this book is *Cancer productus*. The genus name, *Cancer*, means "crab" in ancient Greek, and the species name, *productus,* means "lengthened" in Latin. In cases where there is no common name, just the scientific name is used; if a description refers to many species of the same genus, the genus name is followed by "sp."

## GET OUT AND EXPLORE!

*Before you go:*

- Check a local tide table and plan your visit for about an hour before the low tide.
- Wear closed-toe shoes with good traction: rocks and algae are slippery.
- Wear sunscreen.
- Bring a camera or sketchbook so you can take your memories home.

*When you arrive:*

- Take a moment to watch the waves—the direction they are coming from, where they are breaking. Make sure the incoming tide won't cut off your route back to shore.
- Never turn your back to the ocean: a large wave can surprise you.
- Do not take home animals or shells. Tide pools are fragile ecosystems that need many years to recover from damage, and many tide pool creatures can have

extraordinarily long lives if left unmolested. And unlike those found at the beach, shells in tide pools are rarely empty—they house all kinds of creatures after their original owners die.

- Step carefully. Stay on bare rocks or sand, and avoid stepping on creatures. If you must, tread lightly—mussels and barnacles are tough, but walking on them weakens their shells and attachments, making them vulnerable to the waves.

*Tips for viewing:*

- Slow down, look carefully, and watch patiently to observe creatures and their behavior. Tide pool animals are excellent at hiding and camouflage, but most will come out if they feel safe.
- If you touch something, do it gently, with a wet finger. Poking, pulling, or prying can injure or kill delicate animals.
- If you pick up a rock or an animal, put it back exactly where it was. Some animals stay in one spot throughout their lives—if you remove them, they will not find their way home.
- Enjoy the sights, sounds, and feel of these fascinating places!

# SEA ANEMONES

WITH THEIR CHEERFUL COLORS AND radial symmetry, sea anemones are the exotic flowers of the tide pools. Small animals: beware their lovely petals! Sea anemones belong to the cnidarians (silent "c"), meaning "stinging creatures." Members of this group, which also includes hydroids, corals, and jellies, all have tentacles armed with stinging structures (nematocysts) that ensnare and paralyze prey. An anemone's mouth is located in the center of the creature's oral disk, the area ringed by tentacles. Plankton and organic debris stick to the tentacles and are swept into the mouth; any invertebrates or fishes that can fit in the anemone's mouth are also snatched up. Meals washed onto their oral disks by chance are as welcome as those actively sought, but since the digestive tract has only one opening, the way in is the way out: anemones spit shells and other indigestibles out their mouths.

Nematocysts are dangerous to tiny beasts, but they won't hurt you. If you gently touch a tentacle—with a wet finger, please—you'll feel a little stickiness, but nematocysts from local anemones are too small to penetrate our thick skins. Keep in mind that a nematocyst can only be used once, and the anemone has to grow new ones. Also, the nematocysts from many types of jellies can cause painful stings—never try touching these!

Green-colored anemones (giant greens, aggregating, and sunburst) enjoy a bonus food source: they host tiny algae cells in their tissues. In exchange for a fashionable green hue and a share of the food and oxygen that the algae photosynthesize from the sun, anemones protect algae from snails and other grazers and will even shift into or out of the light to best suit their algae guests. "Green" anemones that live in shade are, despite their name, whitish since they can't support algae.

An anemone clings to rocks with its adhesive foot, or basal disk. While they prefer to stay put, most anemones can glide around underwater, though they are quite sluggish. Hungry sea spiders, nudibranchs, snails, crabs, fishes, and sea stars all prey on them.

Distressed anemones pull their delicate crowns of tentacles inside their bodies to protect against predators as well as the desiccation perils of low tide. Since they are almost all water, they can even contract down to a flattish button of tissue, but it takes a tremendous amount of energy and effort to do so. Closed anemones look like innocuous blobs of goo. Watch out for them! If you step on one, it will squirt out the water it desperately needs to survive until the next high tide.

All anemones can reproduce sexually, producing eggs or sperm and usually releasing them into the water, but some have evolved novel means of asexual reproduction (cloning) that allow them to occupy available space quickly.

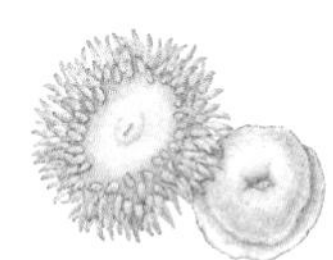

## GIANT GREEN ANEMONE

(to 10 inches across / low intertidal to subtidal)

In deep tide pools, these "old men of the sea" live out long lives: giant green anemones have clocked in 80 years in captivity and might be able to eke out 150 in the wild. Choice real estate for them is under a mussel bed, the better to catch any loose mussels. Their tentacles, sometimes pink-tipped, guide meals to their mouths across smooth, stripeless oral disks. Look for velvety bumps all over their bodies.

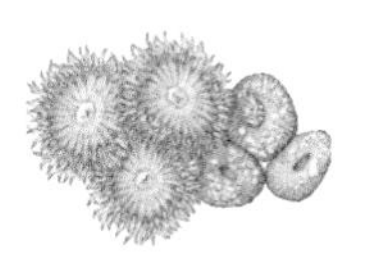

## AGGREGATING ANEMONES

(to 2 inches across / mid-intertidal to subtidal)

Squishy, wet-looking sand may belie a colony of aggregating anemones. The anemones attach sand and bits of shell to vertical rows of sticky bumps on their bodies to ingeniously camouflage themselves, protect against water loss, and shield themselves from the sun. If they're open, you'll see handsome radiating stripes on their oral disks. An aggregating anemone can stretch its basal disk to breaking point, splitting itself into two clones, which will each grow and in turn split, forming a colony. This colony will continue to grow until it runs out of food or space, but if it comes into contact with another colony, the anemones will battle with special, short, white fighting tentacles, full of nematocysts. To avoid combat, they declare neutral zones—you'll see a narrow space separating colonies.

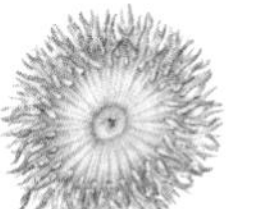

## SUNBURST ANEMONE

(to 10 inches across / mid-intertidal to subtidal)

Sunburst anemones can be as large as giant green anemones, but radiating lines on their oral disks quickly set them apart from their stripeless look-alikes. And while they

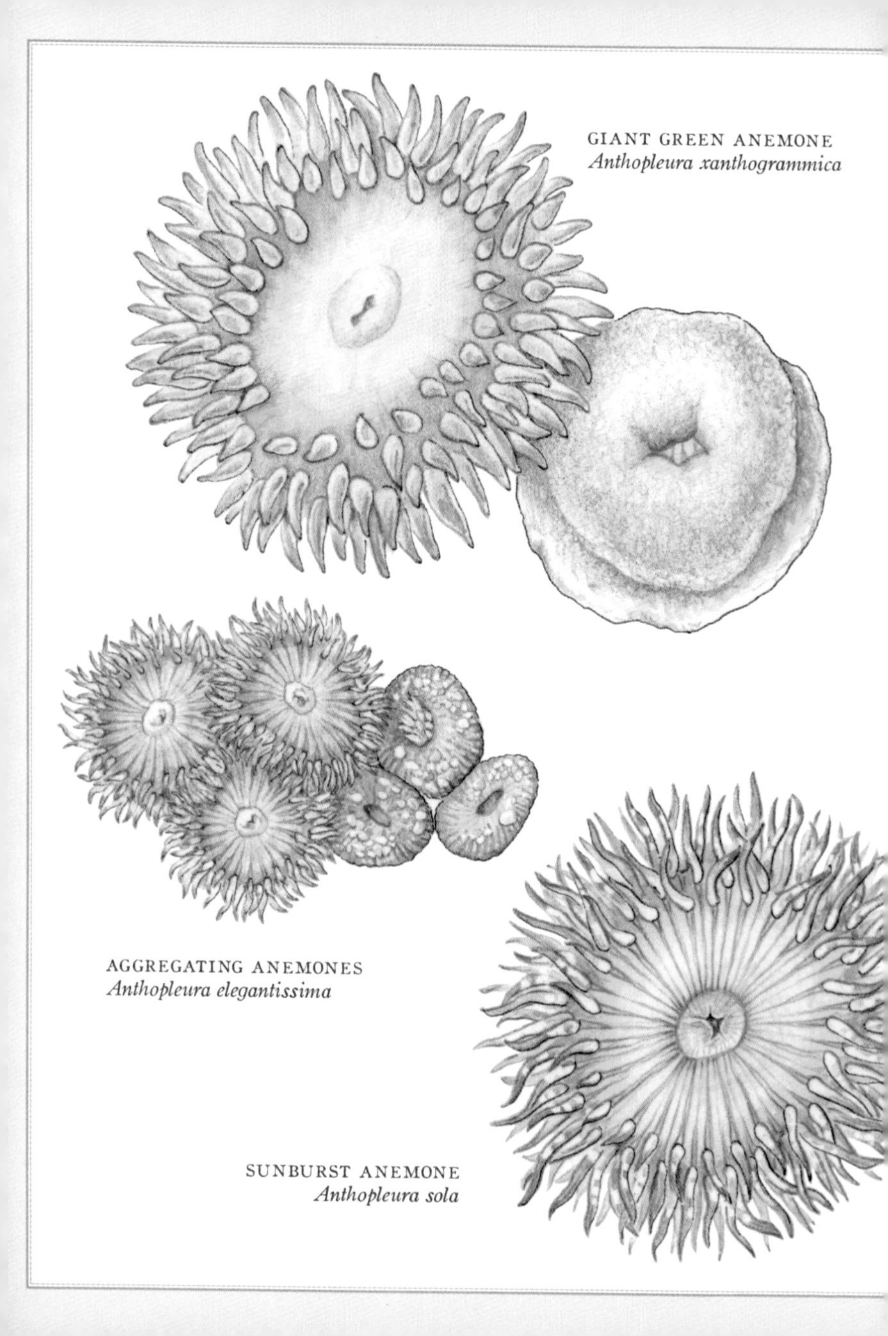
GIANT GREEN ANEMONE
*Anthopleura xanthogrammica*
AGGREGATING ANEMONES
*Anthopleura elegantissima*
SUNBURST ANEMONE
*Anthopleura sola*

# • SEA ANEMONES •

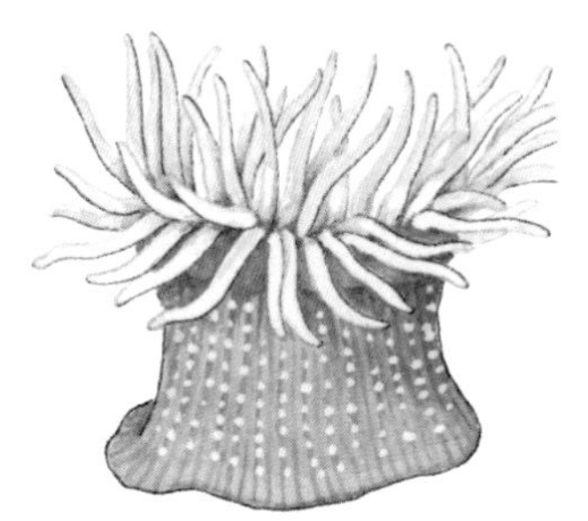

WHITE-SPOTTED ROSE ANEMONE
*Tealia lofotensis*

FRILLED ANEMONE
*Metridium senile*

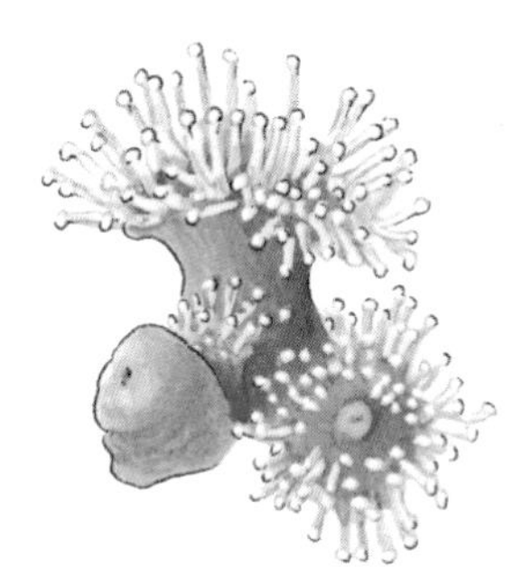

STRAWBERRY ANEMONE
*Corynactis californica*

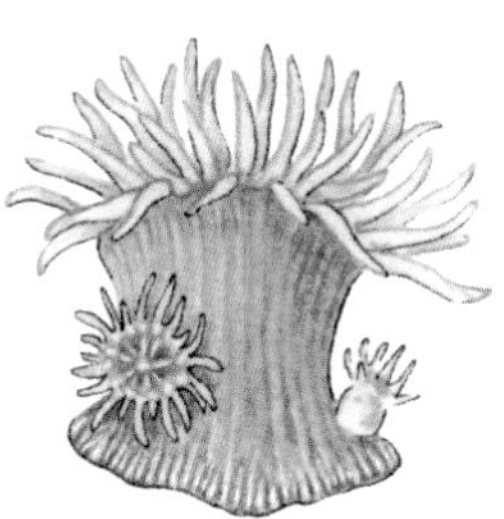

BROODING
ANEMONE
*Epiactis prolifera*

share aggregating anemones' vertical bumps and camouflage techniques, sunbursts prefer a solo existence.

### WHITE-SPOTTED ROSE ANEMONE

(to 5 inches across / low intertidal to subtidal)

Tidy rows of white, wartlike bumps adorn a white-spotted rose's smooth, red body. Juvenile painted greenlings, a type of fish, seem immune to this anemone's nematocysts—they rest among the tentacles or near the base for protection and shelter.

### FRILLED ANEMONE

(to 12 inches tall / low intertidal to subtidal)

This beauty comes in many colors, from white to pale orange to brown, and sports a fringe of fine tentacles atop its long, smooth body column. Small individuals may grace the tide pools, but deeper-water brethren generally grow larger. If attacked, this species flings out long, threadlike filaments packed with nematocysts from its mouth and body to entangle predators in painful silly string. Frilled anemones can reproduce asexually by leaving behind small bits of their basal disks as they creep along; each regenerates, blooming into a new anemone.

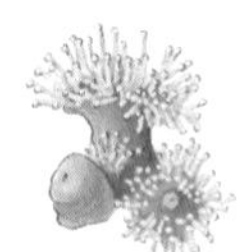

### STRAWBERRY ANEMONE

(to ¾ inch across / lower mid-intertidal to subtidal)

These diminutive anemones—which are found in bright orange, pink, lavender, or tan hues—compensate for their small stature with distinctive, white, club-tipped tentacles that contain extra-large nematocysts. Like aggregating anemones, strawberry anemones can split into clones and form large colonies, but they prefer deeper water and you'll usually only find a few of them in the intertidal zone.

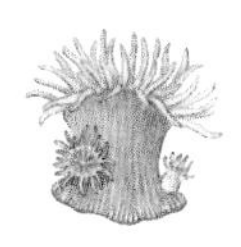

### BROODING ANEMONE

(to ¾ inch across / lower mid-intertidal to subtidal)

This striking little anemone comes in red, green, brown, and gray, but all have bright white radiating lines on their oral disks and distinctive light and dark stripes on the edges of their basal disks. Unlike most anemones, which broadcast their eggs out into the water, brooding anemones keep their eggs inside their bodies until they are fertilized. The larvae then move out their mother's mouth and affix themselves to her "skirt," where they live until they are large enough to crawl off and live on their own. In another reversal, a brooding anemone starts out life as a female, but when it gets to a certain age and size, it develops testes and spends the rest of its life as a hermaphrodite.

# SPONGES

You might notice the small patches—or even large sheets—of color on rocks and in crevices, but you probably wouldn't think they were *animals!* Sea sponges are simple creatures: with only a few cell types, most can't move and don't respond quickly to their environment. However, they are a successful group of animals evolutionarily: they have been around for well over 500 million years and live all over the world, from the icy poles to the tropics.

Sponges have no mouths but are covered with small pores that suck seawater inside. The sponge strains out small food particles, then pumps the filtered water through a large opening (the osculum) at the top of its body.

Because they don't have protective shells or a way to move to wetter places, sponges need to live in the low intertidal to subtidal region, where they are almost always under water. Some sponges grow on other animals: one type of sponge uses chemicals to bore holes into mollusk shells and then grows into the hole, getting a nice safe home and a free ride.

Look for pieces of abalone shell riddled with small holes—this is the work of boring sponges, which generally live in deep water (so are not listed below) but whose handiwork is seen all over the intertidal.

Bath sponges and the small sponges used by artists are the skeletons of sea sponges, but if you bathe with a loofah, you are scrubbing with a fruit, a type of cucumber!

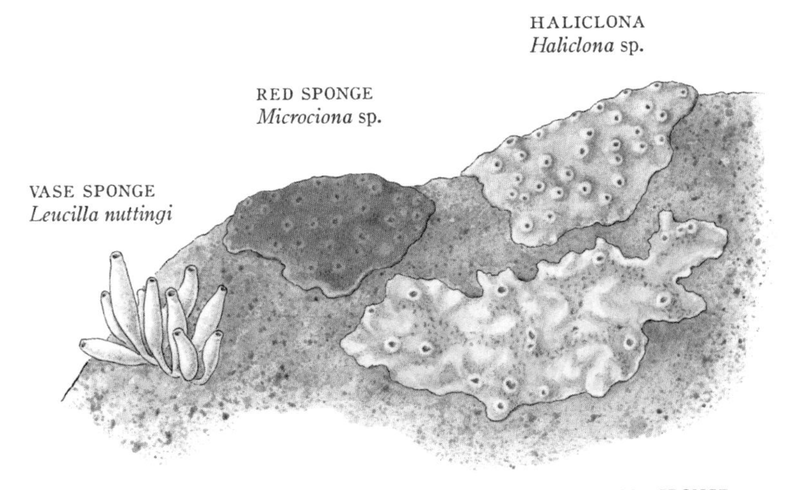

Except for the vase sponge, the species described below grow in masses or colonies of many individuals.

### VASE SPONGE

(up to 1¼ inches tall)

Small, stalked vase sponges are white to cream-colored. They are usually found in small groups, nestled between algae and other invertebrates.

### RED SPONGE

(in mats up to ½ inch thick)

This bright red sponge provides the minute red sponge dorid, a nudibranch (sea slug), with food and a camouflaged home where it can safely lay its eggs. The sponge feels firm to the touch, and its small oscula are flush with the surface.

### *HALICLONA*

(thin sheets 1/16 inch thick)

Tan or purple and spongy-feeling, *Haliclona* has regularly spaced oscula that are raised and tubular, like tiny volcanoes. It can live higher in the tidal zone than any other sponge.

### BREADCRUMB SPONGE

(to 4 inches thick)

The breadcrumb sponge can grow into large masses with thick, irregular surfaces, a sandy texture, and a distinctive sulfurous odor. Some are cream-colored and bread-like, but tide pool forms are often unappetizingly greenish.

# MOLLUSKS

DID YOU KNOW THAT SNAILS and octopuses are closely related? Both are mollusks, a huge group of animals that also includes slugs, mussels, clams, oysters, limpets, chitons, and squids. Mollusks are so diverse that it is difficult to characterize them meaningfully. All of the following are mollusks: passively stuck mussels quietly filtering the water for food; rough-tongued chitons, limpets, and snails unhurriedly grazing rocks for algae; dog whelks drilling pristine holes to feast upon the fleshy interiors of other mollusks; and whip-smart octopuses snatching prey in a flurry of tentacles. Suffice to say that mollusks are well represented in tide pool communities!

## GIANT PACIFIC OCTOPUS

Adult giant Pacific octopuses can reach a hefty thirty-three pounds. They live in deep water, but if you're lucky—not only because they're rare but also because they can change the color and texture of their skin to blend in with their surroundings—you'll see young octopuses in tide pools. Speed, well-developed vision, high intelligence, and eight arms with double rows of suckers make them fearsome predators to shrimps, clams, lobsters, and fishes—sometimes even sharks and birds! A female octopus lays her eggs in grapelike clusters attached to the wall of an underwater cave. She does not eat, but stays with the eggs, blowing water over them and caressing them to keep them clean and oxygenated until the tiny octopuses hatch. She dies shortly afterward.

## CALIFORNIA MUSSEL

(to 8 inches long / mid- to low intertidal)

Mussels have two shells, which they can squeeze tightly together to hoard moisture and bar predators. When the tide is up, a mussel opens its shell and lets the water flow through, filtering food through its breathing gills.

Mussels congregate in large "beds" in high surf zones, gluing themselves to the rocks with tough, flexible byssal threads, which they form by secreting a liquid that hardens upon contact with water. They can withstand years of pounding waves (up to twenty if they're lucky!), and the nooks and crannies of their beds become safe havens for the worms, crabs, small anemones, baby sea stars, and snails that find shelter and moisture there.

Mussels are the preferred meal of sea stars, their main predator. The mussel's only defense is its shell: a sea star needs time to pull it open and the mussel can tolerate longer periods without water than the sea star can; at low tide, a sea star must retreat.

# SNAILS

The smallest whorl at the tip of a coiled shell is the first whorl secreted by the baby snail. The shell provides protection from predators, sun exposure, wave action, and desiccation. For even more protection, many marine snails have a tough, oval-shaped operculum, which they can close like a little door to seal the shell at its opening.

A marine snail is a lot like the snail that lives in your garden, except it has gills and its foot grips very tightly, else it would get washed out to sea by crashing waves. Besides a pair of tentacles with eyes at the tips, most marine snails have additional tentacles for smell, taste, and touch.

## DOG WHELKS

(to 1¼ inch / high to mid-intertidal)

These pretty snails may be yellow, orange, brown, or purple, with stripes and banding. They eat barnacles and mussels by forcing their tubelike proboscis—a long, thin, mouth tube—in between shells (they can drill a hole first if they need to), releasing enzymes to liquefy the prey's body, and sucking up the meal. In rock crevices, dog whelks lay yellow vase-shaped capsules full of eggs. Only a small number of the several hundred eggs are fertilized, and the hatchlings eat the unfertilized ones!

## ABALONE

(5 to 12 inches / subtidal)

Abalones are big snails with flat shells. Each has an enormous muscular foot, like a huge suction cup. Along the edge of the

# · MOLLUSKS ·

*octopuses · snails · limpets · nudibranchs · chitons*

KEYHOLE LIMPET
*Diodora aspera*

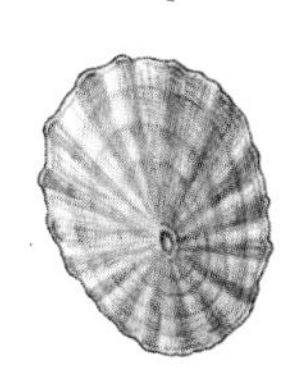

OWL LIMPET
*Lottia gigantea*

BLACK KATY CHITON
*Katharina tunicata*

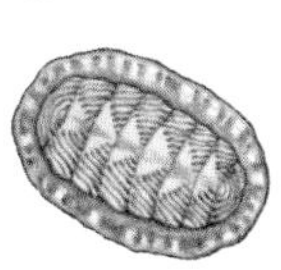

LINED CHITON
*Tonicella lineata*

MOSSY CHITON
*Mopalia muscosa*

ROUGH LIMPET
*Lottia scabra*

RIBBED LIMPET
*Lottia digitalis*

GUMBOOT CHITON
*Cryptochiton stelleri*

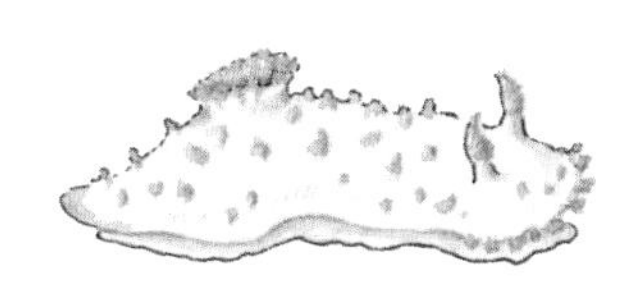

SEA CLOWN NUDIBRANCH
*Triopha catalinae*

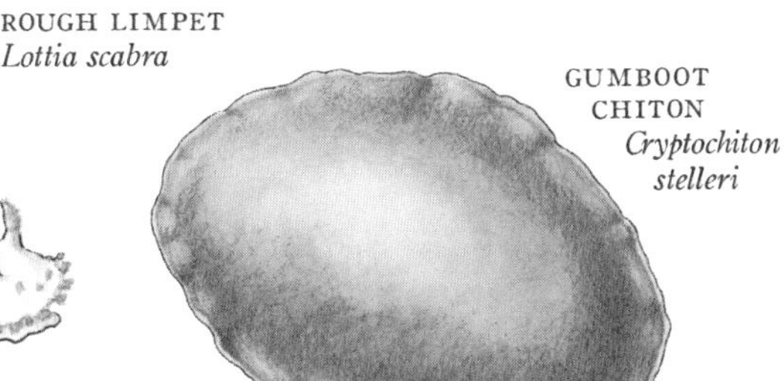

SHAG RUG NUDIBRANCH
*Aeolidia papillosa*

OPALESCENT NUDIBRANCH
*Hermissenda crassicornis*

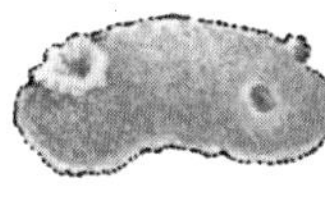

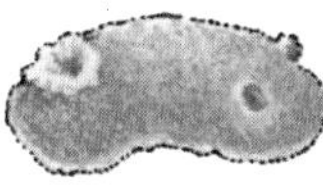

*Rostanga pulchra*

PACIFIC SEA LEMON
*Anisodoris nobilis*

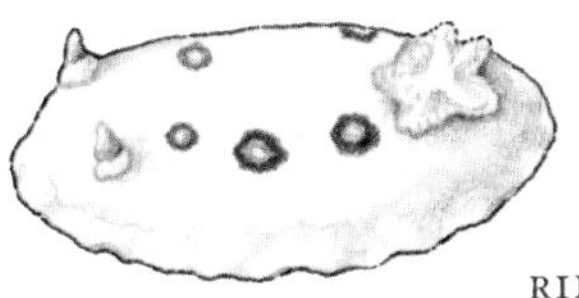

RINGED DORID
*Diaulula sandiegensis*

shell is a row of holes that let water flow out, past the gills; as the abalone grows, it adds new holes. The smooth inside of the shell is a miracle of iridescent color, the result of a pearly secretion that helps protect the abalone's delicate body.

## PERIWINKLES

(to ¾ inch / high to mid-intertidal)

These tough little snails can live in the highest, driest parts of the intertidal, where they graze algae and cluster into crevices to stay moist. Their smooth, dark shells may be brown, purple, or black, sometimes with banding or checkerboard patterns. They often fall prey to sea stars.

## BLACK TURBAN SNAIL

(to 1¼ inch / lower high to mid-intertidal)

The black turban snail's sturdy black or purple shell is a favorite of hermit crabs. If you pick up a shell, hold it gently on your palm and wait patiently to see what emerges: a black foot and tentacles, or lots of little crab legs. This algae-loving snail might reach the ripe old age of thirty if it can avoid the unwanted attention of sea stars and crabs.

## BROWN TURBAN SNAIL

(to 1 inch / lower mid-intertidal to subtidal)

Found in deeper pools than black turban snails, brown turbans have tall, heavy, light-brown shells, often adorned with hitchhikers, like algae or small limpets.

# LIMPETS

A limpet shell is like a domed hat instead of a coil, and with its small head and large foot, a limpet can hug surfaces tightly, both in high tide zones where it's dry much of the time and in the crashing waves of heavy surf zones. Compare the shells of limpets in different places: where battered by rough swells and the hot sun, shells are weathered and damaged, whereas shells in protected areas retain brilliance and color.

Many limpets will also painstakingly scrape rock until they achieve a depression that perfectly accommodates their shell. This "home scar" traps water and gives them a lower profile, making it harder for predators and waves alike to wrest them from their rocks. Under cover of night, the limpet will venture a short distance to forage, usually for algae, always leaving a mucus trail so it can find its way back to its hard-won home.

## KEYHOLE LIMPET

(to 2¾ inches / high to mid-intertidal)

The keyhole limpet has a small hole at the top of its shell, but it's not for access. Rather, it expels water drawn from underneath the shell, past the gills and out this opening. When a sea star attacks, this ingenious limpet raises its shell and extends its soft, slippery body up and around the shell so the sea star can't get a grip. Sometimes a scale worm that lives inside the shell comes to the limpet's aid and bites the sea star as well!

### RIBBED LIMPET

(to 1¼ inch / high to splash zone)

Ribbed limpets tend to live in the high tide zone, on vertical rock faces, clustered in groups to retain moisture. Since they don't make home scars, they settle in a different area after each low tide.

### ROUGH LIMPET

(to 1½ inch / high to splash zone)

Rough limpets are closely related to ribbed limpets, even living in the same high tide zone, but they've no need to compete for space: a rough limpet prefers horizontal orientations and lives alone, returning to its home scar after feeding.

### OWL LIMPET

(to 4 inches / high to mid-intertidal)

This giant limpet is one of the few farmers of the tide pool: it clears an area of rock and lets a thin layer of algae grow there. It grazes on its crop, always leaving some algae behind to grow. And it isn't about to share: using its shell like a bulldozer, it protects its algae farm from invasion by other snails, mussels, and barnacles—though many of these creatures may be found growing on the owl limpet's shell! There's more room for guests on the back of a female; owl limpets are born male, and as they grow older and larger, they become female.

# NUDIBRANCHS

Nudibranchs, or sea slugs, are hands down the loveliest, most vividly colored denizens of tide pools, on average much more glamorous than their landlubber cousins. Like many exquisite things, they are rarely beheld: though there are many types of nudibranchs that live along the Pacific coast, they are often difficult to find—consider yourself lucky if you spot one of these unclad beauties! "Nudibranch" (rhymes with swank) means "naked gills," and without a shell for protection, nudibranchs need deeper water than their shelled relatives; all live in the low intertidal to subtidal range. Two types of nudibranchs are covered below, and the difference is in their gills. Aeolid nudibranchs' gills are scattered along the tops of their bodies in projections called cerata, whereas dorids sport retractable plumes of gills.

Nudibranchs are hermaphrodites: any two can mate and both will lay spiral ribbons or squiggly coils (depending on the species) of eggs, often color-coordinated with the parent. Microscopic larvae hatch from the eggs, complete with their own tiny shells. After swimming free in the open ocean for a few weeks, a larva settles, drops its shell, and metamorphoses into a tiny nudibranch. Alas, beauty fades fast, and like elegant flowers, adult nudibranchs are short-lived, from a few weeks to a year at most.

## RED SPONGE DORID

(to ½ inch)

This wee nudibranch, usually less than half an inch long, perfectly matches the bright red sponges on which it lives and feeds. But the red sponge dorid doesn't seem to need this impressive camouflage, after all: it secretes a substance that most sea stars, nudibranchs, crabs, and fishes find totally unappetizing.

### PACIFIC SEA LEMON

(to 8 inches)

The shockingly yellow sea lemon is one of the largest nudibranchs, capable of a spine-tingling *eight inches* in length. Most of these sponge-loving critters, which you'll see in tide pools, are much more modest in size, though.

### OPALESCENT NUDIBRANCH

(to 3 inches)

This orange-tipped nudibranch with fluorescent blue stripes is beautiful but aggressive. An active predator, it eats sea anemones and other cnidarians, and smaller nudibranchs—it's a cannibal! Even prospective mates will lunge and bite each other.

Though the opalescent nudibranch does *ingest* the stinging nematocysts of its prey, it doesn't *digest* them: instead, it craftily stores them in the colorful cerata on its back, where this obviously painful mouthful helps deter predators.

### RINGED DORID

(to 6 inches)

White or yellow, with characteristic brown rings, this nudibranch, like other dorid nudibranchs, favors delectable sea sponges.

### SEA CLOWN NUDIBRANCH
(to 1½ inches)

White with orange accents—gill and tentacle tips, bumps, and front-edge fringe—the sea clown, like many nudibranchs, can "swim" upside down on the surface of a pool. It looks like showing off, but it's a clever way to sidestep the obstacle course of a tide pool.

### SHAG RUG NUDIBRANCH
(to 4 inches)

This voracious predator gorges itself on sea anemones; not particularly picky about species, it consumes half to all its body weight each day. Its cerata reflect the color of the anemones it has been eating—white to brownish, dull gray to pink. This conspicuous consumption of nematocysts might be painful were it not for this nudibranch's special protective mucus and its thickened mouth and esophagus.

## CHITONS

Instead of a single shell like a snail, chitons have eight tightly overlapping shell plates, and they can fit in spaces that less flexible species would find awkward.

With a fleshy, muscular foot, a chiton clings tightly to rocks, defying winds to dry it out, waves to pry it loose, or predators, like sea stars, birds, and sea otters, to eat it up. If a chiton can't withstand an assault and becomes detached, it slowly curls into a ball like an armadillo to protect its soft underside.

The chitons described below creep along rocks and graze for algae with tonguelike radulas that have special magnetite teeth. They have no distinct head, eyes, or tentacles, and many blend with their surroundings, making them hard to spot by curious humans and hungry predators alike. Having been around for at least 400 million years, they are one of the most ancient types of mollusks.

### BLACK KATY CHITON

(up to 5 inches / mid- to low intertidal)

The black katy chiton has a sleek, smooth, black girdle (body) through which its plates peek. It can sunbathe longer than other chitons, which prefer to hide underwater and in the shade.

### LINED CHITON

(to 2 inches / low intertidal to subtidal)

The extravagant colors of the lined chiton are coordinated with—and camouflaged by—its preferred meal, pink coralline algae. Blue and black plate stripes and a spotted girdle make this chiton unique and striking.

### GUMBOOT CHITON

(to 14 inches / low intertidal to subtidal)

The hulking gumboot chiton conceals its shell plates under leathery, brick-red skin. It is the largest chiton in the world, sometimes over a foot long! Called a "wandering meatloaf" or "football" by some, this chiton can live up to forty years. After a gumboot chiton dies, its butterfly-shaped shell plates may wash up on the beach.

## MOSSY CHITON

(to 3 inches / mid- to low intertidal)

Stiff, hairy bristles cover the mossy chiton's girdle. Algae, small barnacles, or limpets often grow on its brown or gray-green back, sometimes covering the plates completely. A mossy chiton wanders out to feed at night, then returns to its home range come morning.

# WORMS

THE MARINE ANNELIDS (segmented worms) aren't your typical garden-variety earthworms: some are brilliant-hued; some are free-living, predatory, and jawed; others are reclusive, immobile, and tentacled, snatching food particles from the water. With their long, soft, universally appetizing bodies, worms are intensely vulnerable to wave action, desiccation, and predators. Earthworms survive by retreating to underground burrows; read below for marine worms' clever coping strategies.

## CLAM WORM

(to 4 inches / mid-intertidal to subtidal)

When not out and about, this bristly, iridescent, blue-green worm hunkers down in a snug mucus tube under a stone, on algae, in a kelp holdfast, or in a mussel bed. To hunt, it uses four eyes and a battery of tentacles and antennae to zero in on algae and small prey. Then it projects its white mouthpart outside its body and two strong, horny jaws grasp, tear, and pull at the meal. (The mouthpart is called "eversible" because to leave the body it must turn inside out!)

When clam worms are mature, their bodies change dramatically: their eyes enlarge, they grow swimming paddles, and they swell to bursting with eggs or sperm. Coordinating their timing with the lunar cycle, the worms swarm to the water's surface to spawn around midnight. This is unusual behavior for worms, which normally broadcast eggs and sperm, but this concerted and concentrated technique may be more cost-effective for clam worms. They expire shortly after spawning.

## SCALE WORM

(1 to 2½ inches / low intertidal to subtidal)

This large-jawed, predatory worm has protective brown or green platelike scales. Its flat body easily fits into snug spaces, including folds in the bodies of sea stars and mollusks, or the tubes of other worms, where some scale worms are permanent houseguests, neither helping nor hurting their hosts.

## PLUME WORM

(to 4-inch-long tube / low intertidal)

The plume worm protects its tender body with a stony white tube made from paste it secretes with calcium sacs behind its mouth. The tube curves over the surface of rocks or shells. A crown of bright red and pink feathery tentacles peeks out when the worm is underwater, but it can be retracted with lightning speed when it senses you're near; keep still and it may emerge again. One trumpet-shaped tentacle is a door-like operculum to seal the tube from danger and water loss; the

# · WORMS ·

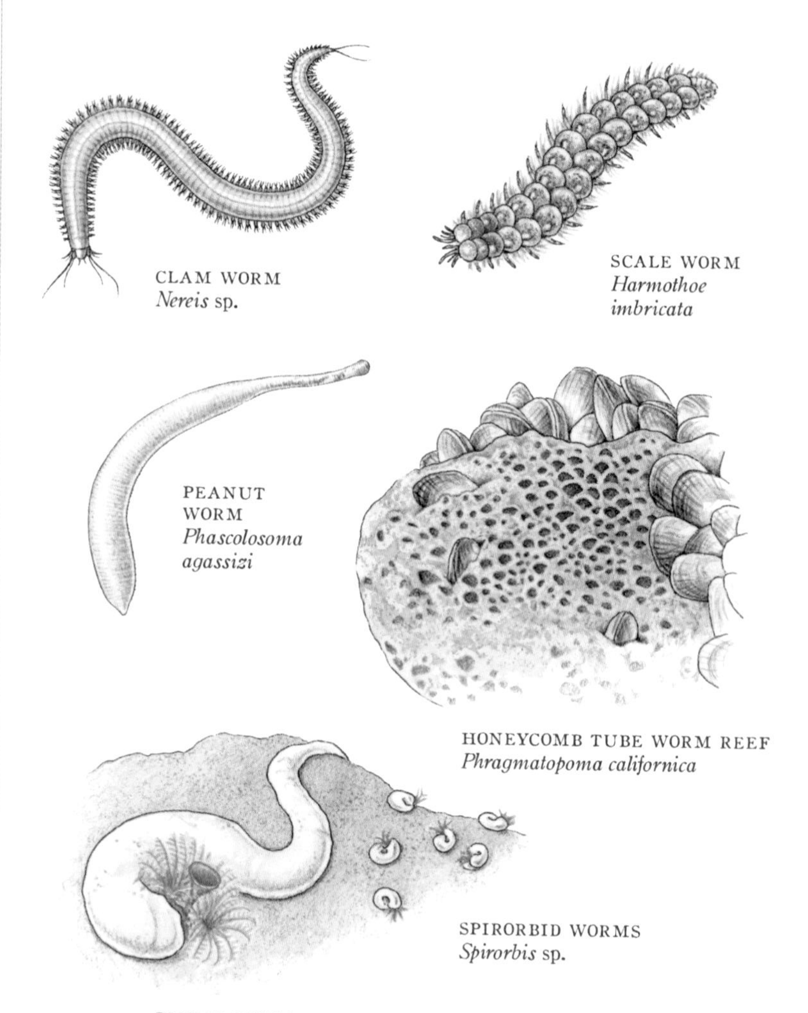
CLAM WORM
*Nereis* sp.
SCALE WORM
*Harmothoe imbricata*
PEANUT WORM
*Phascolosoma agassizi*
HONEYCOMB TUBE WORM REEF
*Phragmatopoma californica*
SPIRORBID WORMS
*Spirorbis* sp.
PLUME WORM
*Serpula* sp.

other tentacles do double duty as gills and filters for food. The ochre sea star is the main predator of plume worms; it jams its shape-shifting stomach right down the worm's protective tube!

### SPIRORBID WORMS

(less than ⅛ inch across / low intertidal to subtidal)

Minute, spiral-coiled white tubes on rocks and shells house this filter-feeding worm. Like plume worms, spirorbids can retract their bright red tentacles in the blink of an eye. Believe it or not, their tubes almost always coil to the left.

### HONEYCOMB TUBE WORM

(to 2 inches long / mid- to low intertidal)

From afar you see a large sandy-colored reef, sometimes several yards wide, but a closer look reveals thousands of individual sand tubes arranged in a honeycomb pattern. You might assume that this is a colony of clones, formed by asexual reproduction; but like many other invertebrates, tube worms reproduce by broadcasting their eggs and sperm, and their gregarious swimming larvae just prefer to cozy up next to others of their kind. When the tide comes up, short purple tentacles grasp for food particles and sand grains. These worms sort the sand grains, keeping the best ones to build and repair their tubes with specially produced liquid cement.

### PEANUT WORM

(1 to 2½ inches long / mid-intertidal to subtidal)

This unsegmented sipunculid worm lurks in crevices and under rocks, in mussel beds and among the roots of surfgrass. It is a deposit, or bottom, feeder with a mouthpiece like an elephant trunk—sometimes as long as the body itself! At the tip of the mouthpiece are eighteen to twenty-four short tentacles that gather food. Often the only part of the worm you will see is this striped mouthpiece; meanwhile, the worm lies safely out of sight in a crevice. When done feeding, the peanut worm turns its "trunk" inside out to retract it inside its body.

# ARTHROPODS

EVOLUTIONARILY, ARTHROPODS ARE A SMASHING success: they live everywhere from the deep sea to the tops of mountains, and they can crawl, swim, and fly. Their ranks include insects, spiders, scorpions, centipedes, and a variety of ocean forms, from microscopic plankton to huge deep-sea crabs.

Arthropods have jointed exoskeletons: tough armor that seals in precious water, protects them from sharp jaws and piercing beaks, and allows them to move quickly and adroitly. Their specialized body parts include tiny mouthparts that can manipulate small pieces of food, shell-crushing claws, nimble running legs, pincers, swimming paddles, wings, and sensitive antennae.

Alas, the exoskeleton does not stretch to allow for growth, and all arthropods need to shed their skin periodically: they take in water and swell up, the old exoskeleton splits at the seams, and the creature crawls out, soft and vulnerable until its new exoskeleton hardens. If you see what looks like a dead crab, try lifting it up—it's probably just an old exoskeleton.

# (MOSTLY) SMALL ARTHROPODS

## ACORN BARNACLES

(to ¾ inch across / high to mid-intertidal)

Like many a tide pool creature, a barnacle starts out as a swimming larva. When it settles, it loses most of its head and glues itself to a surface, using a strong cement that will keep the shell attached long after the barnacle dies. (This cement bonds any combination of materials—of much interest to dentists!) Having established itself, the barnacle also grows a set of shell plates with "doors" to seal water in when the tide goes out. Found on rocks, the bodies of other animals, and even wharves and ships, acorn barnacles don't look like much, but when submerged, they burst alive: their shell plates open and six pairs of feathery legs pop out, beating rhythmically through the water to gather food.

## GOOSENECK BARNACLES

(to 3 inches long / mid-intertidal)

These barnacles' shell plates look so much like little beaks that early Europeans, ignorant of migrating avian life cycles, thought they actually were geese in the making! With shell plates and feeding legs affixed to rocks by a tough, rubbery stalk (the goose's "neck"), this barnacle will stay put even when bashed by strong waves.

Like flocks of birds, gooseneck barnacles occur in clusters, often with small barnacles attached to the bases of large ones for protection. Gooseneck barnacles compete with mussels for the same habitats and food, and they fall prey to some of the same predators: snails, sea stars, and gulls.

## ISOPODS

(to 1½ inches / low intertidal to subtidal)

The familiar pill bugs you find in your garden are isopods—they even have gills! Their ocean-living cousins can't roll themselves into balls, but they are excellent swimmers and very hard to find if they keep still. They are the exact color of their edible home—marine algae or surfgrass—and hang tightly to the algae with strong, pointy legs.

## SEA SPIDERS

(to ⅜ inch across / low intertidal to subtidal)

With their thick, clawed legs bent at odd angles, yellowish bodies with minuscule abdomens, tiny eyes, and huge sucking proboscises, sea spiders are one of the most alien-looking creatures in the intertidal. Their movements are achingly slow, maybe because their bodies are so tiny that each muscle is only a single cell. There is no room in their abdomens for their digestive systems, so their intestines extend to the tip of each leg. They use their proboscises like straws to suck the juices out of soft anemones, small cnidarians, and tunicates. Male sea spiders have a small pair of extra legs so they can carry developing eggs under their bodies. Sea spiders are not true spiders, though related. Sea spiders that live in the deep waters of the Antarctic swell to almost three feet across and can run around on their long, thin legs.

# CRABS

Zipping across a tide pool and dashing back under a cover of rocks or mussels, crabs are lively creatures. Small crabs are a much-loved food of birds, fishes, and many marine mammals, so they are excellent at running and hiding. Their eyes distinguish between light and dark and quickly register approaching shadows. They deftly navigate rocky habitats by way of sensitive antennae and hairs on their legs. Their four pairs of walking legs are too close together to allow them to walk forward—they'd get tangled if they tried!—but they've mastered a darting sideways scuttle. When waves are crashing down or when a predator is trying to pull them out of a crevice, they use their sharp leg tips to hold on for dear life.

Crabs are the cleanup crew of the tide pools, scavenging dead animals, plants, and algae. (Some eat fresh algae or shellfish meals, but all are scavengers.) Their nimble pair of claws allows them not only to manipulate their food, tearing it and picking up tiny bits, but also to protect themselves.

You can tell the difference between a male and female crab by turning one upside down, best done if you can find an empty molt or very gently with a small live crab—larger ones can hurt you! The abdomen is folded underneath the carapace

*Male (left) and female purple shore crabs*

(the crab's shell): it's pointed in males, but wide in females, the better for holding hundreds or thousands of eggs until the swimming larvae are ready to hatch.

The sizes below refer to the width of the crab's carapace. Of the larger crabs described, most tide pool dwellers will be juveniles, much smaller than this measurement.

### HERMIT CRABS

(to ¾ inch across / high intertidal to subtidal)

If you see snails scuttling across the bottom of a tide pool, look again: you are probably seeing incognito hermit crabs. A hermit crab's long, soft abdomen fits perfectly into a coiled shell, to which it holds on with its last two tiny pairs of legs. Hermits actually venture out *more* than their crab cousins, safe in the knowledge that they can pull quickly into their shell for protection. Some hermit crabs prefer particular types of shells, but all need to trade up in size as they grow—and they will fight over good shells if they have to!

### PORCELAIN CRAB

(to ¾ inch across / high to mid-intertidal)

Porcelain crabs are also called "flat crabs," their planed bodies allowing them to fit snugly under rocks, in mussel beds, or in crevices. Just as you would around breakable porcelain, be gentle around these crabs: they will easily drop their broad, flat claws if they are disturbed. Even though its claws can eventually grow back, a crab can't protect itself and its territory in the meantime, which might spell its death sentence. Porcelain crabs will eat algae and scavenge the occasional dead animal, but they mostly filter bits of food out

SEA SPIDER
*Pycnogonum* sp.

ISOPOD
*Idotea* sp.

ACORN BARNACLE
*Balanus glandula*

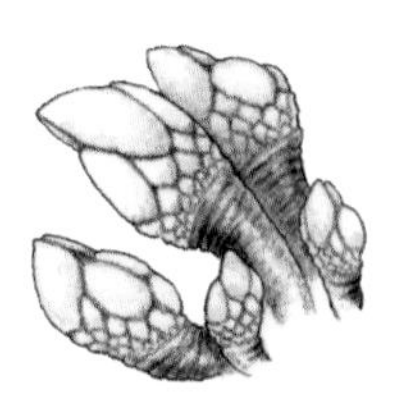

GOOSENECK BARNACLE
*Pollicipes polymerus*

PURPLE SHORE CRAB
*Hemigrapsus nudus*

GREEN SHORE CRAB
*Hemigrapsus oregonensis*

LINED SHORE CRAB
*Pachygrapsus crassipes*

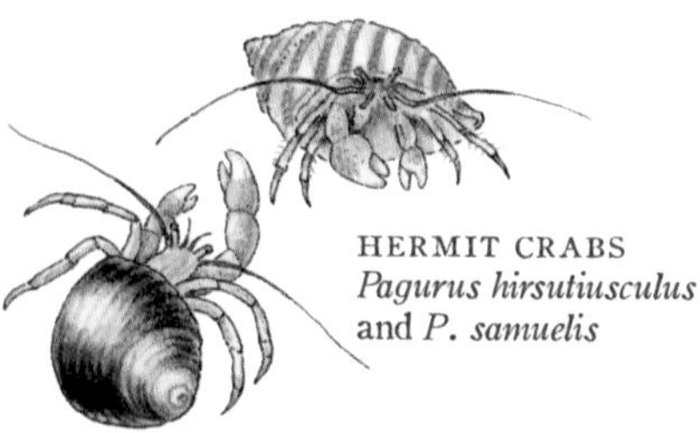

HERMIT CRABS
*Pagurus hirsutiusculus* and *P. samuelis*

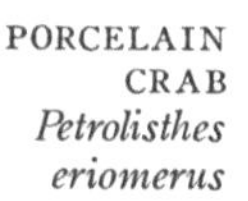

PORCELAIN CRAB
*Petrolisthes eriomerus*

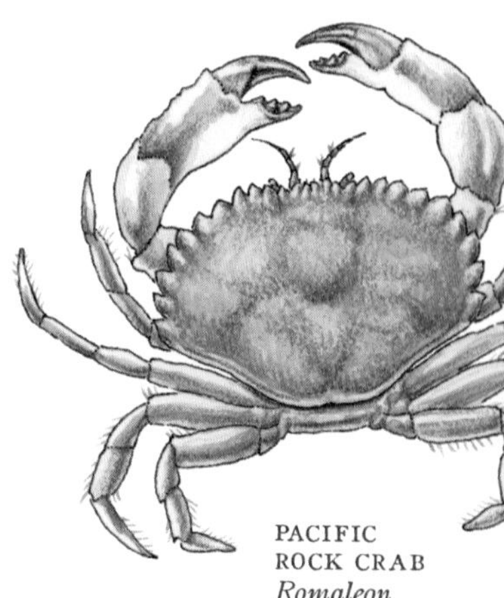

PACIFIC ROCK CRAB
*Romaleon antennarium*

# • ARTHROPODS •

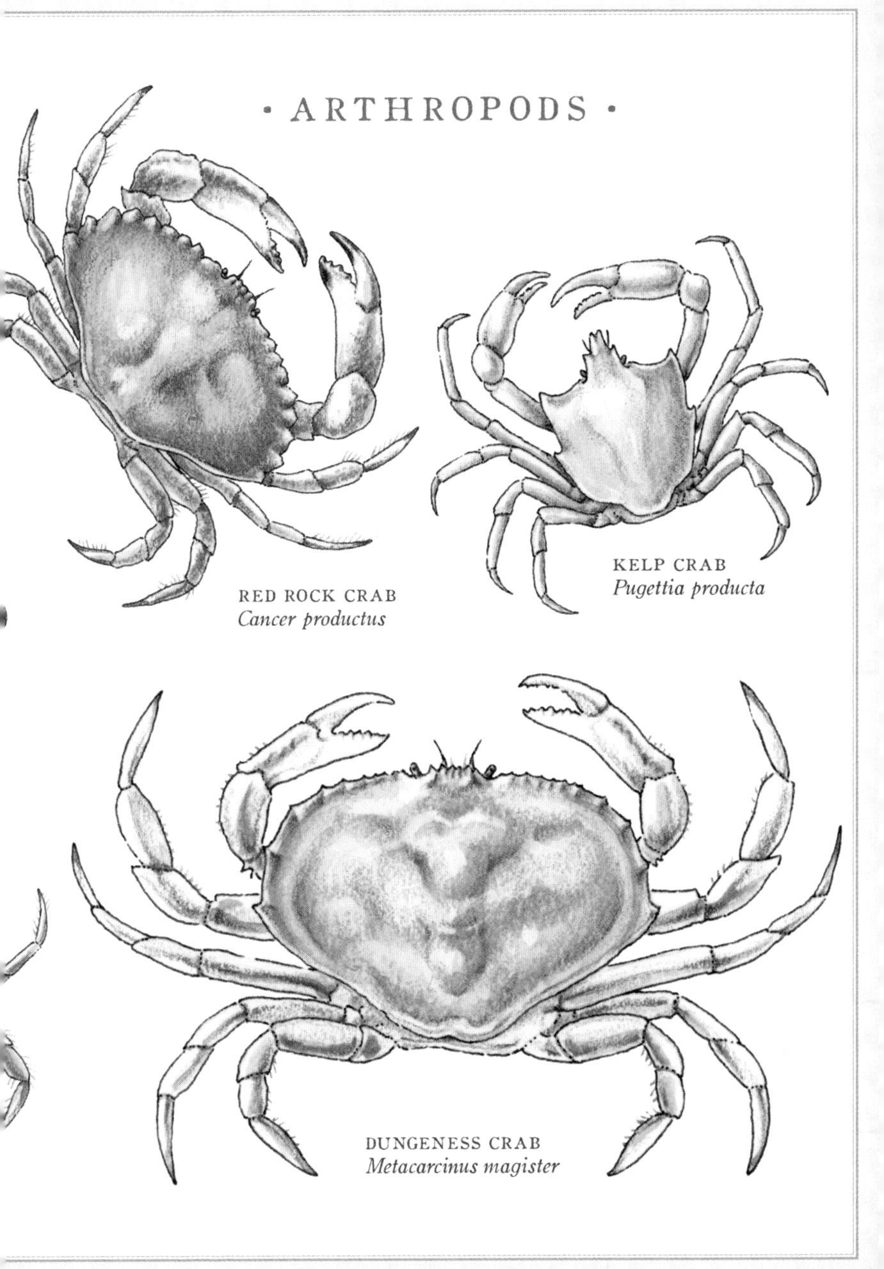

RED ROCK CRAB
*Cancer productus*

KELP CRAB
*Pugettia producta*

DUNGENESS CRAB
*Metacarcinus magister*

of the water with their feathery mouthparts. It may seem that porcelain crabs have only three pairs of walking legs, but the tiny fourth pair is safely tucked up behind the carapace.

### LINED SHORE CRAB

(to 2 inches across / high to mid-intertidal)

These feisty little crabs can stay out of the water longer than other tide pool crabs, so their presence is virtually assured. If you are quiet and still, they might even come out of the hiding spot to which you've sent them scrambling with your approach. With deep purple and green stripes, this crab blends in well as it scrapes small bits of algae off the rocks with its strong claws. If it feels cornered, watch out for those claws!

### GREEN SHORE CRAB

(to 2 inches across / high to low intertidal)

Its dull, yellowish brown or green color and the bristly hairs on its legs differentiate the green shore crab from the similarly sized and shaped lined shore crab and purple shore crab. Besides living under rocks in the intertidal zone, green shore crabs favor sandy and muddy shores, where they blend well and dig burrows.

### PURPLE SHORE CRAB

(to 1½ inches across / mid- to low intertidal)

The purple shore crab is similar in size and shape to the lined shore crab, but it lacks shell stripes, instead sporting purple polka dots on lavender claws. Found a little lower in the intertidal than the lined shore crab, the purple shore crab is a bit slower and more mild-mannered than its pugnacious look-alike.

## KELP CRAB

(to 5 inches across / low intertidal to subtidal)

This handsome specimen has a smooth, shiny shell; small, strong claws; and long, thin legs with sharp tips for grasping the marine algae on which it lives and feeds. Slow-moving and perfectly camouflaged, it can be hard to spot. Large crabs usually live in kelp forests, but young crabs grace tide pools.

## RED ROCK CRAB

(to 8 inches across / low intertidal to subtidal)

When it isn't buried in sand, the red rock crab can be admired for its handsome black-tipped claws and brick-red shell, potential home to a dizzying array of hangers-on, including barnacles, sponges, tunicates, algae, and worms. The female must be soft-shelled to mate, and a hopeful male will guard a female until she molts and then protect her while her shell hardens; in turn she will protect the 150,000 or so eggs on her abdomen until the swimming larvae hatch. Juvenile crabs may have intricate red and white zebra stripes.

## PACIFIC ROCK CRAB

(to 7 inches across / mid-intertidal to subtidal)

This large crab is similar to the red rock crab, with dark tips on stout claws and a smooth red shell. Its long, prominent antennae are the main distinguishing feature, unless you want to get closer to look at the spots on its underside or start counting the teeth on the carapace (eleven on each side outside the eyestalks)—a dangerous undertaking, as these crabs can break snail and mussel shells with their claws and may do some serious damage to fingers!

### DUNGENESS CRAB

(to 9 inches across / low intertidal to subtidal)
This large, reddish brown to purple crab has white-tipped claws with spiny ridges and yellow legs fringed with short hairs. The females lay up to 2.5 million eggs, and the larvae will sometimes attach themselves to jellies, on which they feed, protected from predators, while being transported to new habitats.

# ECHINODERMS

A STARFISH ISN'T A FISH! It is more properly called a sea star and belongs to the echinoderms, a group of hearty marine animals that also includes brittle stars, sea urchins, sea cucumbers, and sand dollars. All are radially symmetric (usually pentaradial, or five-part) and starlike; all are, true to their name, "spiny-skinned." Besides spines, many echinoderms also have minuscule pincers that move around on short stalks to help clean and protect the echinoderm's surface. You won't see other invertebrates parking on their backs.

Echinoderms move, breathe, capture food, and attach by means of an amazingly intricate hydraulic vascular system of fluid-filled canals connected to tiny bulbs which are in turn connected to flexible tube feet. To move, the echinoderm contracts a bulb, and the corresponding tube foot floods and thus extends. Disks at the bottom of the tube feet secrete strong glue that sticks to surfaces, and if you pull on an animal that's firmly attached, you will tear off its tube feet—ouch!

Most of the echinoderms you will see in tide pools will be sea stars, which come in a dazzling array of shapes and colors. A sea star's eyes, able to detect light, are on the tips of its arms, and the anatomical whimsy doesn't stop there. See that small, round, usually light-colored area on the sea star's top surface, just off-center? That's its madreporite, where water enters its water vascular system. Its mouth is located in the center of its underside, and when it's time to eat, a sea star pushes its inside-out stomach *out of its mouth.* Sea stars' reproductive strategies are less shocking, their spawning typical of marine invertebrates: eggs and sperm are usually released directly into the water, and fertilization produces swimming larvae that feed and grow until they metamorphose to adults.

Because of their tough, spiny skin, sea stars aren't appetizing to most creatures; the main threat to sea stars is humans, specifically collectors and ill-mannered tide poolers.

Except for the ochre sea star and six-rayed sea star, which can tolerate the mid-intertidal, sea stars are found in low intertidal to subtidal ranges. Each measurement below represents the diameter of the whole animal.

## OCHRE SEA STAR

(to 16 inches across)

The most familiar Pacific coast sea star, with spiny white bumps and orange, brown, or purple skin, ochre sea stars are the scourge of mussels. They camp near the bases of rocks, often under mussel beds, where they can stay moist. When the tide comes in, the sea star uses its sticky tube feet to climb up and hunker down on its chosen mussel victim. Mercilessly pulling on both shells, the sea star will persist for hours until the mussel gets tired, finally relaxing and loosening the smallest bit. The sea star thrusts its inside-out stomach from its mouth and through the shell gap of the exhausted mussel, which is liquefied by digestive juices. The sea star slurps up its hard-won meal, one of about eighty mussels it will consume in a year.

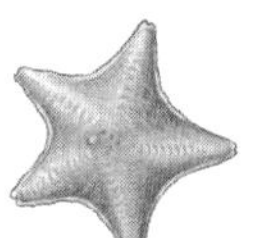

## BAT STAR

(to 8 inches across)

With its short arms and broad central disk, this star seems to have webbed bat wings, though its coloration doesn't follow suit: bat stars come in a rainbow of hues, from white with orange blotches to yellow, orange, red, purplish, blue, or green. Their tube feet are not as strong as other sea stars', so they must forgo shelled mollusk meals and stick to the bottoms of pools, where they scavenge or content themselves with meals of surfgrass.

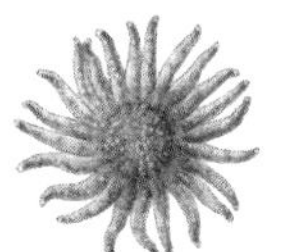

## SUNFLOWER STAR

(to 40 inches across)

Large (the largest in the world!), many-limbed (up to twenty-four from its original baby six), and ridiculously fast (up to six feet per minute), the voracious sunflower star would utterly dominate if other invertebrates hadn't evolved a flight response to its smell. Red, orange, or purple, sunflower stars do have a softer side: their bodies are more pliant and flexible than those of most other sea stars.

## LEATHER STAR

(to 11 inches across)

A leather star has spineless, leathery gray skin covered with clusters of orange-red spots that function like gills. One type of anemone, at least, knows better than

# • ECHINODERMS •

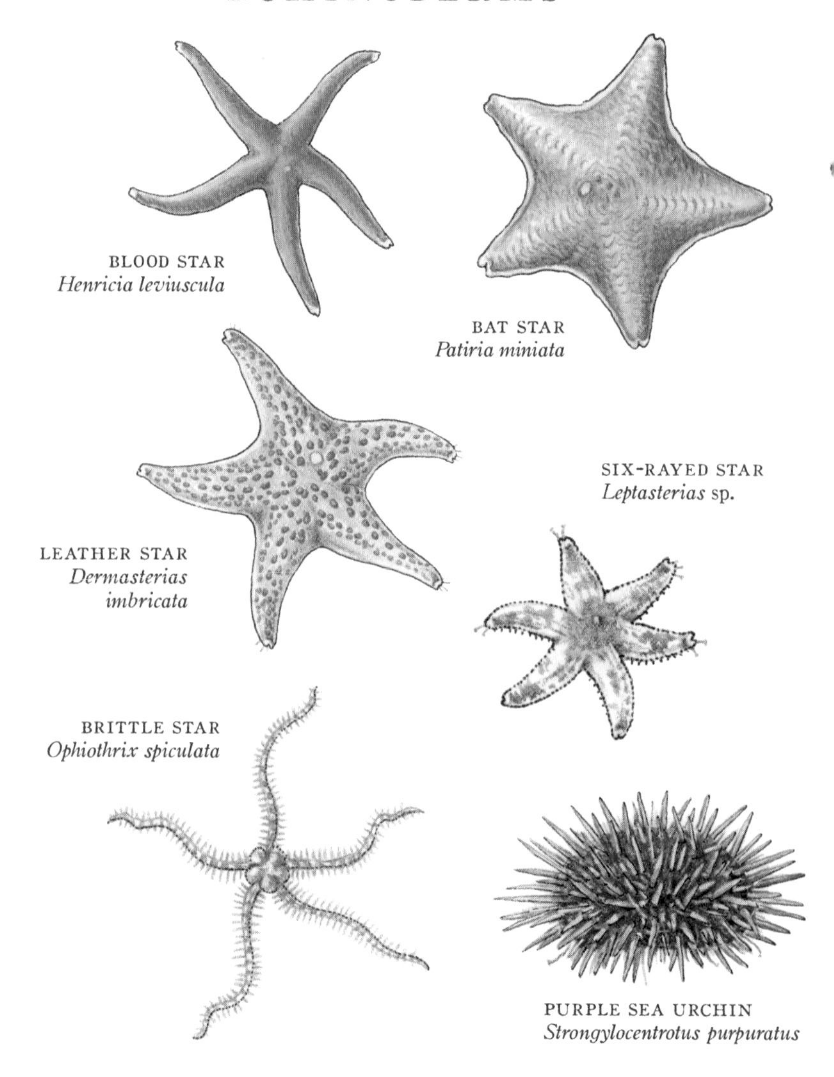

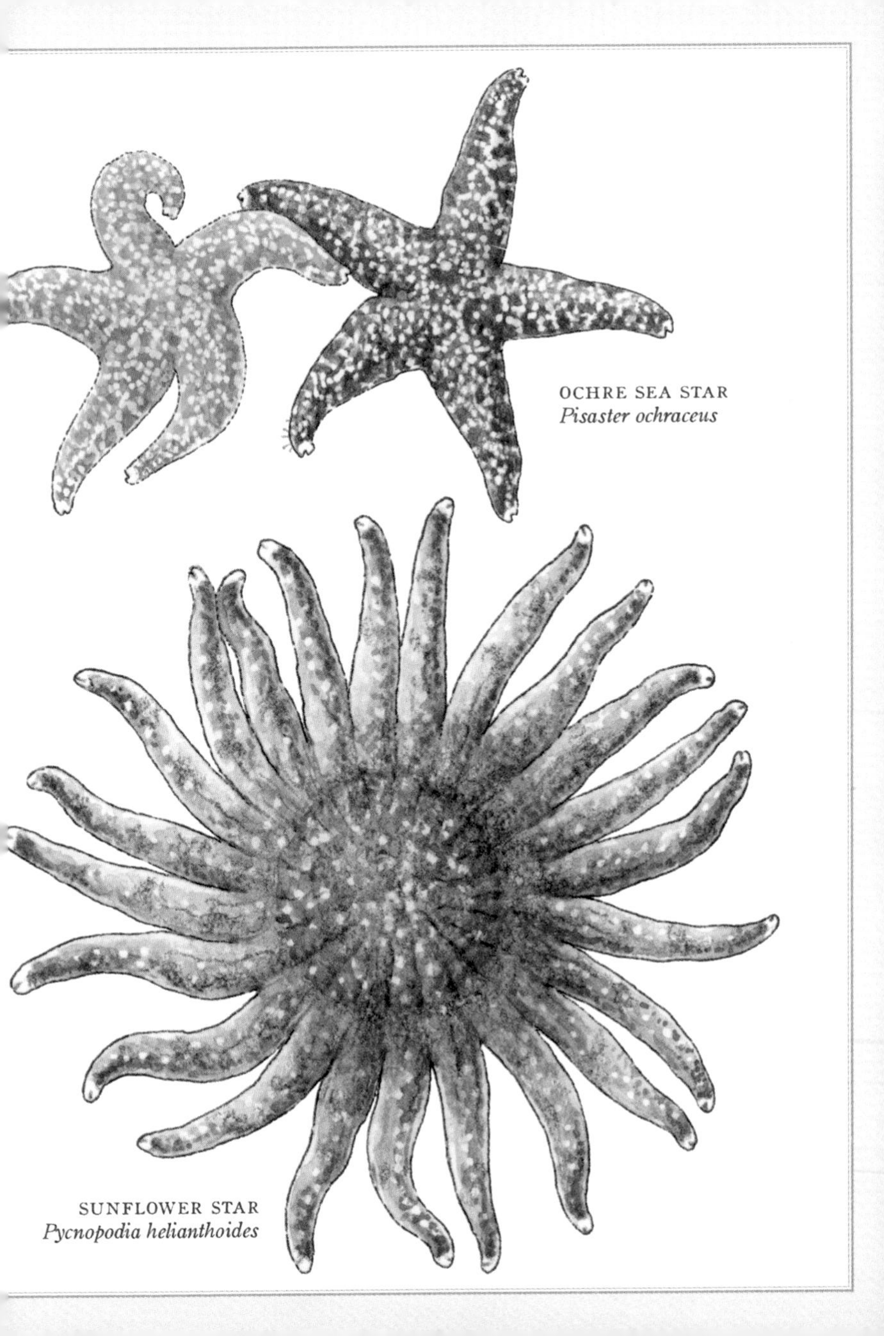

OCHRE SEA STAR
*Pisaster ochraceus*

SUNFLOWER STAR
*Pycnopodia helianthoides*

to stick around after this star's approach: it will detach from the rocks and swim away, likely tipped off by the star's garlic/sulfur odor. Luckily (for leather stars), they also enjoy sea cucumbers, urchins, and other anemones.

### SIX-RAYED STAR

(to 4 inches across)

In spite of its name, which *is* accurate on average, a six-rayed star might have five or seven arms. Of mottled green or reddish purple hue, it clings very tightly to rocks with its myriad tiny tube feet and competes with the larger ochre star for food and tidal zone. The female is a self-sacrificing mother, brooding her yellow eggs near her mouth, where they block her from eating and from attaching to rocks properly: she must hang on by the tips of her arms. Eggs that don't get washed away hatch into tiny (less than ⅛ inch) babies.

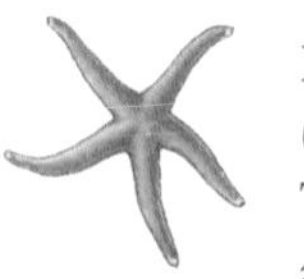

### BLOOD STAR

(to 5 inches across)

The blood star's gruesome name refers to its usually brilliant orange-red color, which, along with its slender arms and smooth, spine- and pincer-free skin, makes it easy to spot in a tide pool. A predator of sea sponges, the blood star also traps bacteria and small food particles with mucus.

### BRITTLE STAR

(to 12 inches across)

There are many species of brittle stars, all with central disks and long, snakelike arms. Instead of creeping around on tube feet like sea stars, brittle stars propel themselves by slithering their sinuous arms. They hide in crevices, under rocks, or in sand, extending their arms out to entrap small worms or crustaceans and to collect bits of food from the water. Many a tide pooler mistakes these little arms for worms. When a brittle star is attacked, its arm will break off; the star escapes, and a new arm will eventually grow back. In places where many brittle stars flock, their searching arms look like fields of grass.

## PURPLE SEA URCHIN

(to 4 inches across, not including spines)

The bony plates that make a sea star's skin tough are enlarged and fused together to form a rounded shell in the sea urchin. Sea urchins also have tube feet, though theirs are longer and more slender, and their significantly longer spines and pincers also assist locomotion. Spines, pincers, and tube feet can all be used as utensils to grab bits of algae to transfer to their mouths; a special set of jaws with five strong teeth can scavenge, scrape algae off rocks, or take chunks out of the sea urchin's favorite meal, giant kelp. Where a rock is soft enough, a sea urchin uses its jaws and spines to carve out an ingenious cubbyhole. Besides being a great place to hide, the hole fills with water at low tide and turns into a mini tide pool. Urchins often cover their bodies with shells, rocks, and algae, further reducing water loss, protecting themselves from the sun, and enhancing their camouflage.

Touch an urchin's spines—gently, they're pointy!—and other spines will move toward your finger to better defend the urchin. But even with their sharp spines and nipping pincers, sea urchins have plenty of predators. Sea otters especially enjoy them; their bones become stained purple if they eat enough of them. Crabs, anemones, and fishes will eat urchins if they get the chance, and sun stars can swallow sea urchins whole.

# TUNICATES

THESE JELLY-LIKE MASSES YOU SEE on rocks have been through an amazing transformation, unheard of anywhere else in the animal kingdom: they go from being proto-vertebrates to something else entirely. In its larval stage, a tunicate swims about, tadpole-like, and has a nerve cord and primitive spinal column. But it can't eat! So it finds a suitable spot and cements its head to it, never to leave. Then it undergoes a radical body reorganization: it absorbs its own tail, along with its primitive brain, eye, and nerve cord. The gills turn into siphons—one to draw in water and filter plankton and other organic matter (incurrent), the other to expel water and waste (excurrent). A "tunic"—which ranges from cartilage-like to gelatinous depending on the species—forms around the new body, and the creature spends the rest of its days pumping water. How's that for settling down?

Tunicates come in three varieties: solitary, social, and compound. Solitary species might be found in groups, but that's only because a larva parked next to an adult. Social and compound aggregations comprise genetically identical clones, the main difference being whether or not they share a common tunic. (If they do, they're compound.) Compound tunicates look a lot like sponges, a colorful layer growing on the rock. To tell the difference, touch gently: compound tunicates are firm and slippery, while sponges have a texture like felt. Peer closely and you will see the tiny individuals within the shared tunic—unlike a sponge, which has only small pores covering its surface.

There are a few species of sea stars, worms, and snails that feed on tunicates, but many tunicates produce chemicals that discourage potential predators.

Tunicates are also called "sea squirts": if upset, some species will shoot water from both siphons, to the delight of children and children at heart. But tunicates don't tolerate desiccation well and are found only in low intertidal and subtidal ranges.

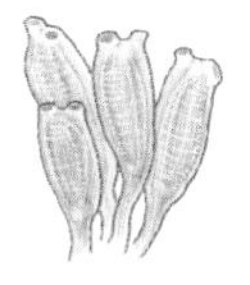

### LIGHT BULB TUNICATE

(to 1½ inches long)

A thin, transparent tunic with two bands of bright pink tissue, used for feeding but resembling light-bulb filaments, gives this charming tunicate its name. This social species is clustered on rocks; look for new buds, or clones, at the base of a cluster. Light bulb tunicates brood their eggs in the summer, and their bright orange larvae can be seen inside their see-through tunics.

### STALKED TUNICATE

(to 6 inches long)

The solitary stalked tunicate wears a pinkish brown, grooved, and leathery tunic; because of its long, tough stalk, it is undaunted by the roughest waters.

### SEA PORK

(to 1¼ inch thick)

This compound tunicate forms gelatinous, shiny slabs, sometimes several inches wide. Yellow, orange, white, or pork-like pink, these delicate colonies are decidedly absent from wave-pounded areas.

### SANDY SLAB SEA SQUIRT

(less than 1 inch thick)

Brown, reddish, or purple, sandy slab sea squirts are found in thick, firm colonies flecked with grains of sand.

### MUSHROOM ASCIDIAN

(colony to 1½ inches across)

This purple, orange, gray, or yellow compound tunicate creates rounded or mushroom-like colonies; individuals are arranged in small groups, each sharing a single excurrent.

# · TUNICATES ·

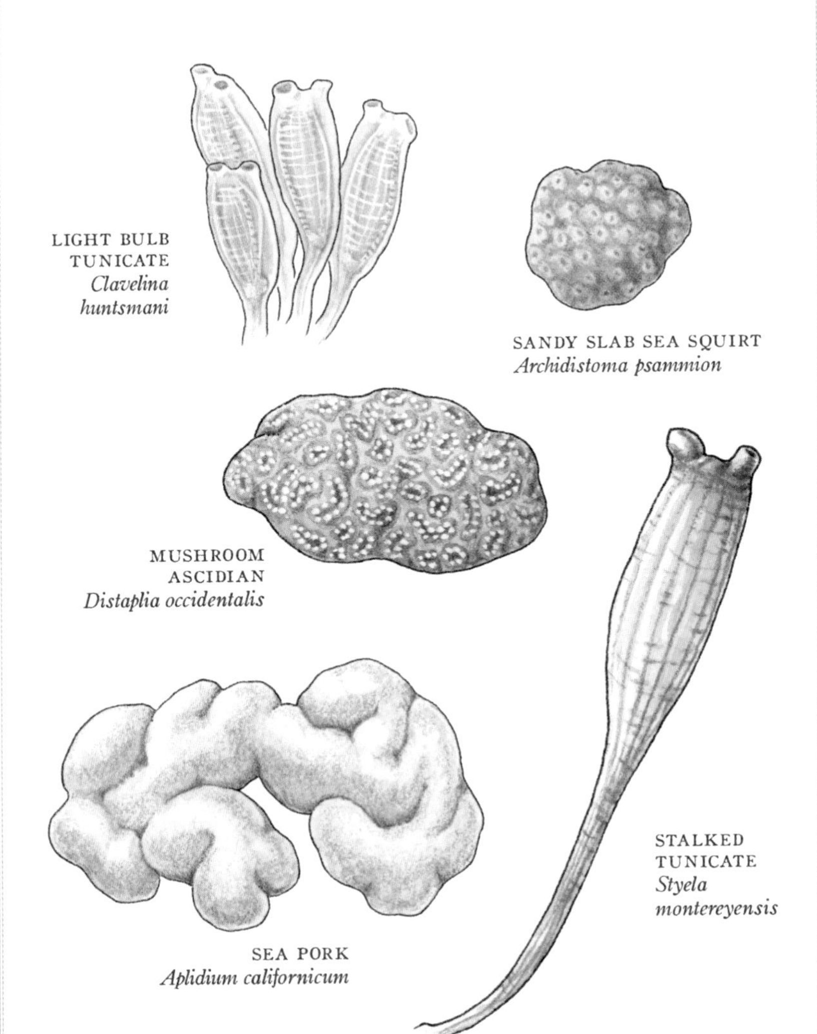

LIGHT BULB
TUNICATE
*Clavelina huntsmani*
SANDY SLAB SEA SQUIRT
*Archidistoma psammion*
MUSHROOM
ASCIDIAN
*Distaplia occidentalis*
STALKED
TUNICATE
*Styela montereyensis*
SEA PORK
*Aplidium californicum*

# FISHES

It takes a special kind of fish to survive the extreme conditions of the intertidal environment, where the presence of water isn't guaranteed. But tide pool fish are well armed for low tide: they can breathe air, survive out of the water for several hours if kept moist, and tolerate extremes of temperature and salinity. Their bodies are specially built for hovering and hiding rather than long-distance swimming. Pricklebacks and gunnels, for example, have small front fins and smooth bodies so they can sidle back into hidey-holes. Masters of camouflage, tide pool fishes often stay perfectly still, and you won't see them unless they move. Most have a special spot under or between rocks that they call home; if you move rocks, please put them back!

## TIDE POOL SCULPINS

(to 4 inches)

All Pacific coast sculpin species have large heads and tapered bodies with red, green, or brown splotches. Pat

# • FISHES •

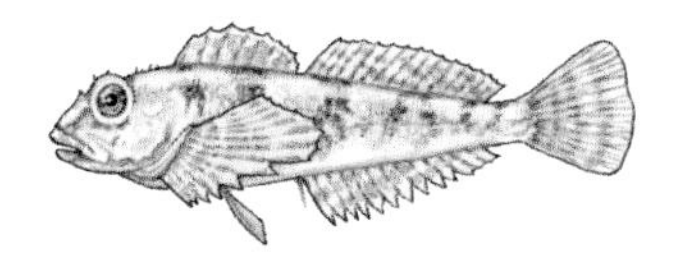

TIDE POOL SCULPIN
*Oligocottus maculosus*

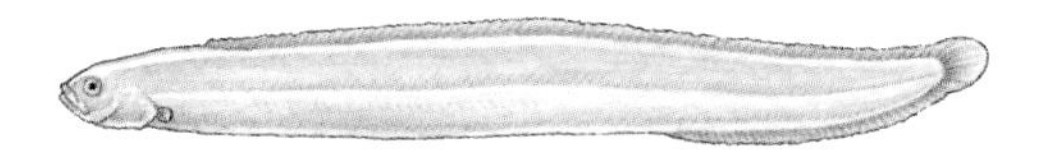

ROCKWEED GUNNEL
*Apodichthys fucorum*

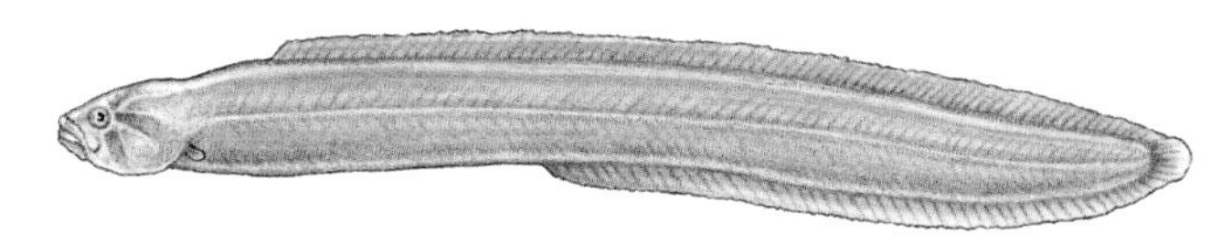

ROCK PRICKLEBACK
*Xiphister mucosus*

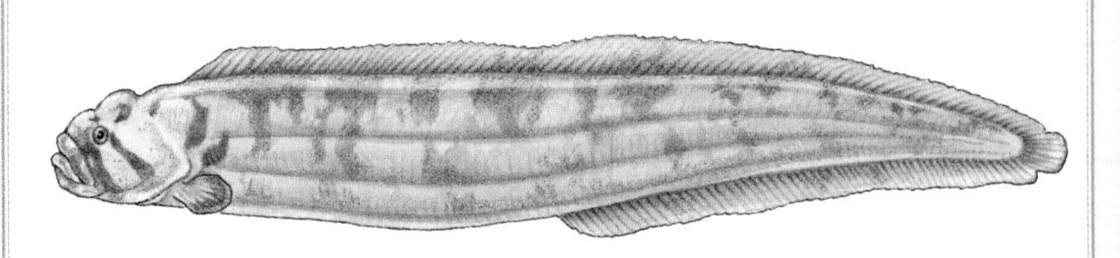

MONKEYFACE PRICKLEBACK
*Cebidichthys violaceus*

yourself on the back if you spot one: this fish disappears into the intricate backdrop of a tide pool with only a streak of movement, revealing that it was there all along. With those bulging eyes atop its head, that sculpin probably saw *you,* though! It has a keen sense of smell, so it can track small prey, sense predators, and even find its way back to its favorite tide pool if it gets washed out by waves. Small invertebrates are prey; birds and larger fish are predators.

### ROCKWEED GUNNEL
(to 9 inches)

Rockweed gunnels share the slender physique of prickle-backs, but on a more petite scale. Translucent green, red, or yellow, their jewellike bodies are well camouflaged with the algae among which they live. These feisty fish are often found in rockweed beds, where they troll for small mollusks and arthropods.

### ROCK PRICKLEBACK
(to 23 inches)

A rock prickleback has a greenish black body and striped face, and its spiny dorsal fin and slimy strategy for staying moist give this species its Latin name *(Xiphister mucosus).* Juve-niles' carnivorous habits mature into a late-life preference for algae—also true of the monkeyface prickleback. Egg masses are laid under a rock, and it's the male prickleback that shields them from harm.

## MONKEYFACE PRICKLEBACK

(to 30 inches)

Confusions abound: even with its thick lips and ridged head, the monkeyface prickleback doesn't particularly resemble a monkey. And though it is often called a "monkeyface eel," this fish is not a true eel! Adults are large enough to deter predation, but young fish are a tasty treat for birds and larger fishes.

# BIRDS

TONS OF BIRDS NEST AND feed near the ocean—to identify them all, you'd need a book devoted to birds. However, there are a few birds that specifically hang out near tide pools and enjoy the smorgasbord of delectables that low tide serves up to them. Birds of the rocky intertidal typically have stocky bodies and are triply adept at swimming, flying, and walking. The birds described below nest on the ground near the water (some gulls nest on cliffs, however); their eggs are tough enough to survive being washed over by waves, and as soon as newly hatched baby birds' downy feathers are dry, they are alert and ready to run.

## GULLS

(14 to 27 inches, depending on species)

Many species of gull live along the West Coast, though they don't always nest by the ocean, which is why ornithologists don't like the overly general term "seagull." Adults are usually a combination of white, gray, and

• BIRDS •
BLACK OYSTERCATCHER
*Haematopus bachmani*
GULL
*Larus* sp.
BLACK TURNSTONE
*Arenaria melanocephala*

black (though they sometimes sport a slightly different look in the winter); juveniles usually have more subdued, mottled brown plumage. These large, brave, and often vocal birds are just as happy to steal part of your picnic as they are to eat crabs, worms, and pretty much anything else.

### BLACK OYSTERCATCHER

(to 17 inches)

Fear not: you couldn't possibly mistake the Black Oystercatcher for any other bird. With its brown-black body, long, red-orange bill, and yellow eyes ringed with red, it's as eye-catching as it is oyster-catching. Its strong beak pries mussels, limpets, chitons, and barnacles off the rocks, and any worms or crabs it finds along the way are also fair game. A noisy bird, the Black Oystercatcher will scold other birds—or you—for getting too close.

### BLACK TURNSTONE

(to 9 inches)

Smaller and more delicate than gulls or oystercatchers, Black Turnstones are distinguished by handsome breeding plumage, with black feathers offsetting a white belly and special white detailing that includes spotting, feather tips, "eyebrows," and a patch in front of the eye. In the winter, their look is more toned down—dark brown without spots and eyebrows, more in line with their juvenile days. The pointed, slightly upturned beak easily pries barnacles and limpets open. On a sandy beach, the "turnstone" will do just that: turn stones, shells, or algae over, looking for little creatures to eat.

# MARINE ALGAE

WASHED UP ON THE BEACH or growing on the rocks, marine algae, often called seaweeds, are a feast for the senses with their rich colors, salty ocean scents, and slimy stickiness. Some are even edible, tickling our taste buds after proper preparation. From microscopic to lush forest forms, marine algae anchor the ocean's food chain, and we have them to thank for a large percentage of the oxygen we breathe.

The marine algae that you see in the intertidal *look* like plants, but because the algae live in the ocean, the way they function is quite different. A plant has roots that anchor it and bring water and minerals up from the soil, nutrients which must then be transported to the other parts of the plant. The holdfasts of marine algae may look like roots, but their purpose is simply to grip the substrate; because all parts of marine algae are bathed in water and minerals and can absorb them, there is no need to transport these nutrients.

Plants and marine algae both photosynthesize, using energy from the sun to convert carbon dioxide and water into oxygen and sugars, but while plants accomplish this exclusively with their leaves, pretty much the entire structure of marine algae—not just the leaves, or "blades"—can manufacture nutrients.

Because water is denser than air, marine algae don't need to support their own weight like plants do—the water does it for them, and you'll notice that most marine algae are limp and flabby when removed from the water. Even so, the blades of some species are connected to a stemlike stipe, which allows the algae to grow large or to edge closer to the light. Some marine algae have gas-filled air bladders that float like little balloons, bringing the algae to the water's sunlit surface.

The first thing you notice when you touch a marine alga is that it's slippery or downright slimy. Absorbent gel-like substances keep the algae from drying out when exposed to the air, and along with their rubbery, tough, and flexible parts, this allows marine algae to withstand the abuse of the intertidal and glide over—rather than be shredded by—rough rocks and sharp invertebrates.

Most marine algae have complicated life cycles with at least two phases, one when they produce eggs and sperm, and another when they produce spores. The phases sometimes look completely different from each other.

There are three different groups of marine algae, based on the types of pigments that they use for photosynthesis: green, brown, and red. Green algae probably gave rise to plants many millions of years ago. There are marine, freshwater, and terrestrial species of green algae—some even grow on the surface of snow! Brown and red algae are almost all ocean dwellers.

When you are looking at marine algae, watch for intertidal invertebrates tucked between blades, clinging to stipes, and nestled into holdfasts. Like most specimens of subtidal species, tide pool algae are often much smaller than sizes listed here.

# GREEN ALGAE

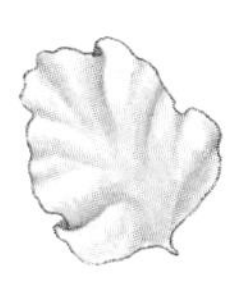

## SEA LETTUCE

(to 3 feet long / high intertidal to subtidal)

This vivid green alga grows in rippled clusters of thin, transparent sheets, each just two cells thick. Tolerant of brackish water, sea lettuce will grow high in the intertidal zone in the runoff from streams or storm drains. A bare rock won't remain so for long if the colonizing sea lettuce is around; along with marine bacteria and diatoms (microscopic algae with intricate, glass-like shells), it coats rocks with a nutritious algal film much loved by grazing mollusks. Tiny sea lettuces will grow on blades of surfgrass.

## PIN CUSHION ALGAE

(to 5 inches across / high intertidal to mid-intertidal)

Lustrous green and densely packed with branched fibers, the pin cushion alga looks like clumps of moss and acts like a kitchen sponge—it can hold a lot of water, helping it survive long stretches of time out of water. Minute periwinkles are often tucked into the algae, where they bask in the moisture.

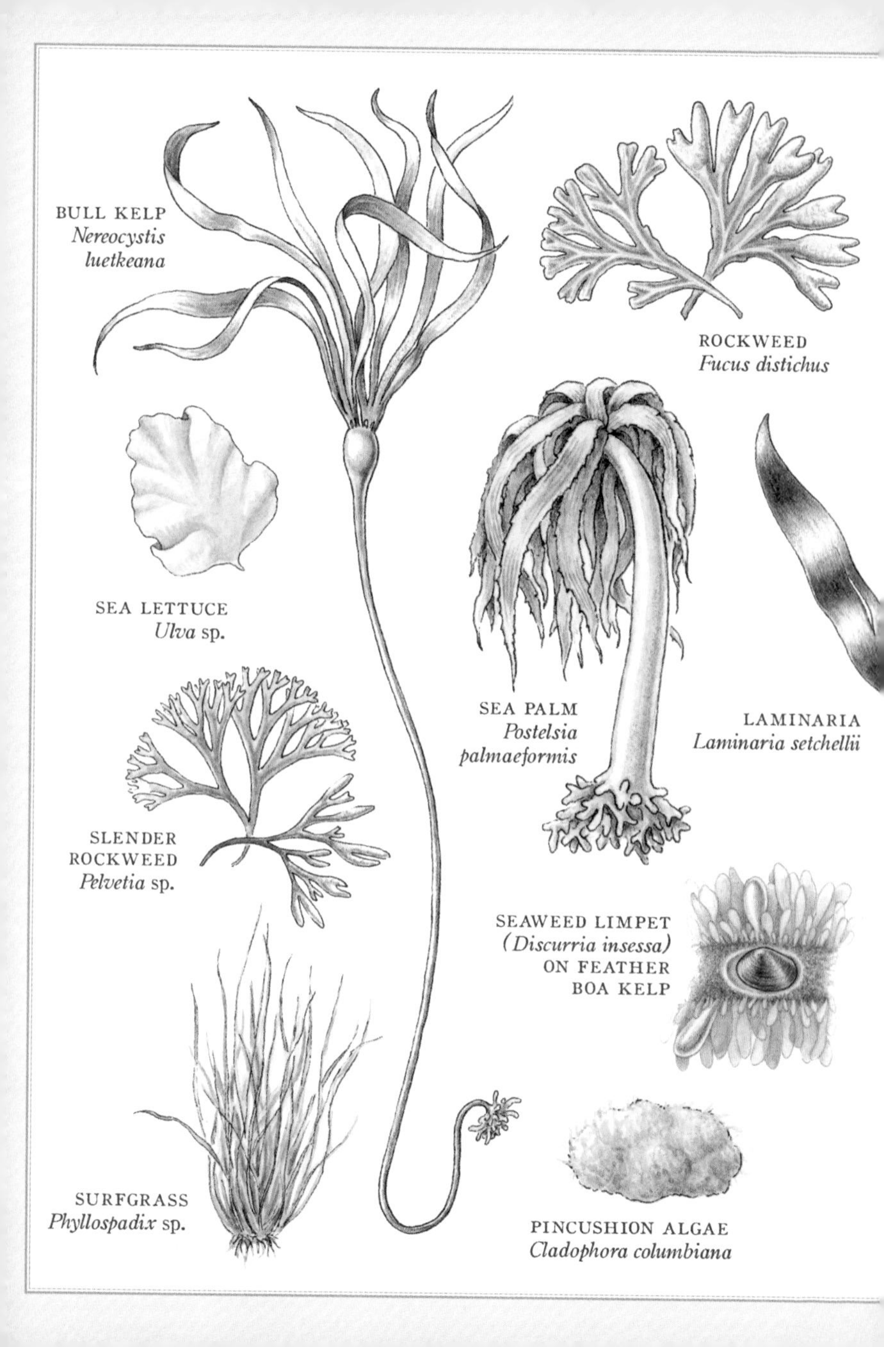
BULL KELP
*Nereocystis luetkeana*
ROCKWEED
*Fucus distichus*
SEA LETTUCE
*Ulva* sp.
SEA PALM
*Postelsia palmaeformis*
LAMINARIA
*Laminaria setchellii*
SLENDER ROCKWEED
*Pelvetia* sp.
SEAWEED LIMPET
*(Discurria insessa)*
ON FEATHER BOA KELP
SURFGRASS
*Phyllospadix* sp.
PINCUSHION ALGAE
*Cladophora columbiana*

# • MARINE ALGAE •

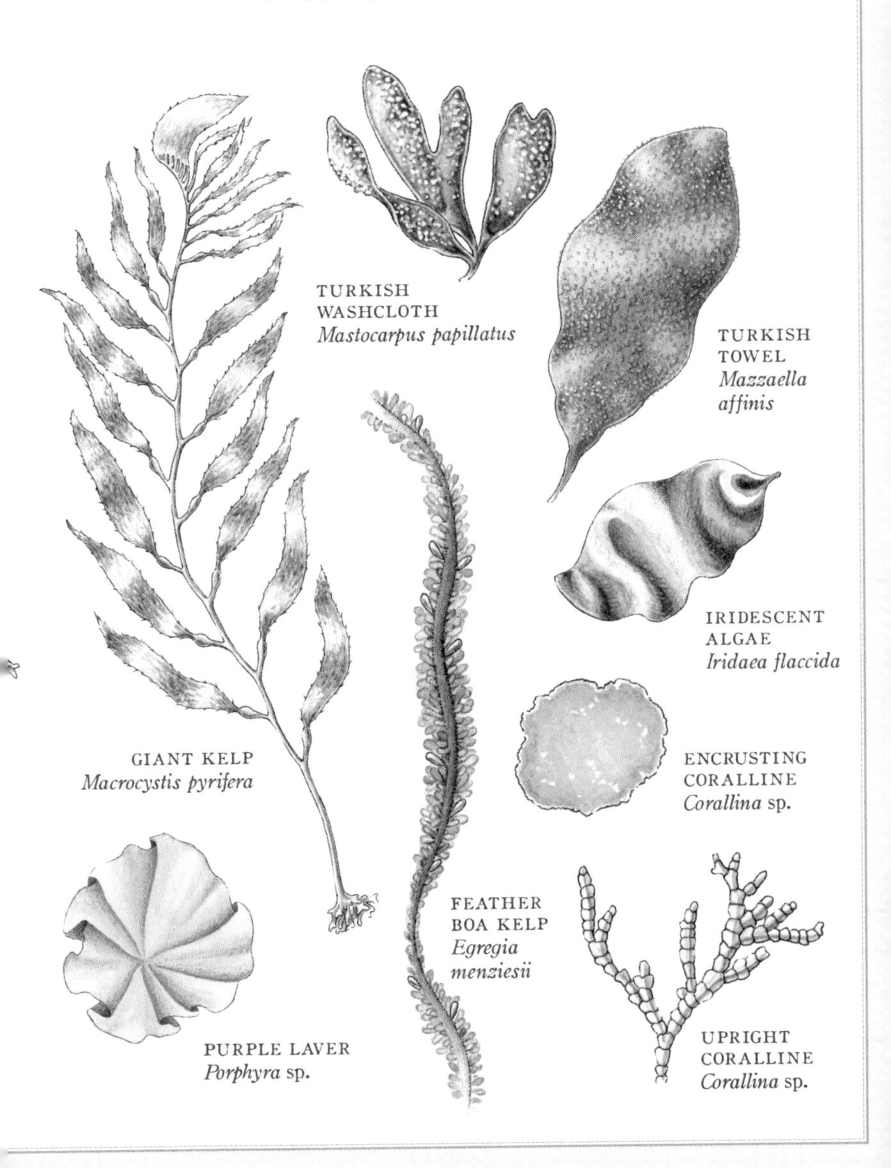

# BROWN ALGAE

Brown algae encompass microscopic forms to enormous kelps that form vast underwater forests anchored offshore with stipes reaching over one hundred feet from the sea floor. Each large holdfast is home to hundreds of tiny creatures, and the many long blades form a dense canopy that provides food and shelter for invertebrates, fishes, birds, and marine mammals. Alginic acid, also called algin or alginate, is the gel-like substance in their cell walls that makes brown algae slippery. We use it as a thickener or emulsifier for printing, paper and fabric production, dentistry (making impressions of your teeth), pharmaceuticals, cosmetics, and food (ice cream, jelly, soup, salad dressing, etc.)—most of us use alginic acid every day!

## ROCKWEED

(to 12 inches long / high intertidal to mid-intertidal)

Rockweed has broad, flat, and gooey olive-brown blades with raised midribs. They are arranged in neat dichotomous branches, meaning that each branch point offers up a pair of twin branches. Their holdfast is strong but small, and their swollen branch tips house reproductive structures and allow them to float along the surface for better photosynthesis.

## SLENDER ROCKWEED

(to 5 inches long / high intertidal to mid-intertidal)

Slender rockweed grows high in the intertidal, where it retains precious water, and if you poke through its yellow-brown and midrib-less blades, you'll find a whole host of creatures staying wet and cool. If the blades turn black and crispy from severe desiccation, all that's needed is a splash of waves, or even just a heavy fog, for it to rehydrate and look as good as new.

### *LAMINARIA*

(to 3 feet long / low intertidal to subtidal)

You'll see this brown alga nodding on its tough, upright stipe as the waves wash back and forth. Its one blade, smooth and shiny, is often deeply divided, offering less resistance to the force of the waves than a single large blade would. *Laminaria* can live between twelve and twenty years if it isn't overgrazed.

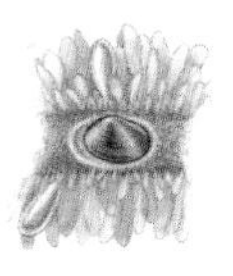

### FEATHER BOA KELP

(to 30 feet long / low intertidal to subtidal)

With its feathery blades and bulbous floats affixed to a flattened, strap-like stipe, feather boa kelp does make a lovely—if sticky—fashion accessory. Its holdfast is incredibly strong, as is its stipe—feather boas grow in surge channels with a lot of ocean force. Look closely at a stipe for a glimpse of the seaweed limpet, which is found only on this type of algae. It sports a tall, smooth, shiny brown shell (to ¾ inch) and carves deep home scars to protect it from drying out and from wave action. This limpet activity does weaken the stipe, which often breaks at the home scar, but on the other hand it may keep the kelp from growing too long and breaking away at the holdfast.

## BULL KELP

(to 140 feet long / subtidal)

The familiar "bull whip" of the beach, bull kelp has a single long and thin stipe with a large hollow bulb at the end, out of which sprout two tufts of long, thin blades. Bull kelp grows in deep water, at the prodigious rate of up to seven inches a day, but often breaks loose after a rough storm and may be found washed up on shore or in tide pools.

## GIANT KELP

(to 180 feet / subtidal)

Giant kelp has hundreds of trailing blades, each attached to its long stipe by a small float. Along with bull kelp, giant kelp forms the majority of the kelp forests along the Pacific coast. It puts bull kelp to shame in the growth department: giant kelp can grow twenty inches each day, faster than almost any other organism on Earth! Its impressive holdfast may be three feet across and three feet high.

## SEA PALM

(to 2 feet tall / high to low intertidal)

Charismatic sea palms resemble miniature palm trees. Found in areas that receive extreme wave shock, they grow in clusters, often attached to mussels. The substantial holdfast supports the "trunk," a strong, flexible, hollow stipe. Come low tide, the many drooping blades release spores that drip down the blades' grooves onto the substrate, where they attach themselves before high tide to start the "seeds" for a new "forest."

# RED ALGAE

Red algae have the largest number of species, and because their pigments are able to absorb the green and blue-green colors of light that penetrate deepest into the water, red algae can live at greater depths than most other algae.

"Red" algae may actually appear green or purple, depending on what pigments are present in their cells. Reds are a source of carrageenan and agar, used like alginic acid to thicken products such as yogurt, ice cream, soy milk, toothpaste, shampoo, and cosmetics.

## PURPLE LAVER

(to 3 feet / high and mid-intertidal)

If you have ever had dried seaweed snacks or sushi wrapped in seaweed, you are familiar with the subtle taste—salty, almost nutty—of a type of purple laver known as nori. People have been eating purple laver since 500 AD in China, and it is now grown in huge commercial farms. This red alga is incredibly thin, only one or two cell layers thick, but super-resilient. In the intertidal, it can dry out for a few days, turning black and crunchy, but if its gets the tiniest bit of water, voila! The delicate green or purple blades, often lobed or ruffled, bounce back to health. The other stage in purple laver's life cycle is a minute form that bores into mollusk shells and forms a rosy patch of red filaments.

### TURKISH TOWEL

(to 32 inches long / mid- to low intertidal)

"Turkish towel" seems like a strange name for algae until you see them. The reddish purple, unbranched blades are completely covered with a lawn of small bumps, or papillae, that give them a towel-like texture. Tide pool specimens can be several inches long, but in deeper water they can grow to almost towel size! Look for pieces of these washed up on the beach.

### TURKISH WASHCLOTH

(to 6 inches / mid- to low intertidal)

The small, dark red to purple blades of Turkish washcloth are split at the tips and develop papillae when they are reproductive. They grow in dense clusters and don't seem palatable to most herbivores, instead providing a cool, moist place for invertebrates to hang out. The other phase of Turkish washcloth's life cycle is a black crust that looks like a spot of tar on the rocks. Before people understood the complex life cycle, they thought it was a separate species. The tar-spot form is long-lived, up to ninety years, and it produces spores that grow into little washcloths which die back each year.

### IRIDESCENT ALGAE

(to 8 inches long / mid-intertidal to subtidal)

The size, shape, thickness, and color of this red alga differ wildly, depending on exposure to light and waves. Green to purple to black, small or large, when the blades are under water, they are stunningly iridescent, like the surface of a bubble, or oil on water. This rainbow effect is caused by the structure of the outer layer, a multilayered cuticle that may protect the blades from tearing, water loss, and grazing.

### UPRIGHT CORALLINE ALGAE

(to 8 inches tall / low intertidal to subtidal)

This red alga, with its pink, segmented branches, looks like a tiny tree dipped in Pepto-Bismol. Rock-hard cell walls are impregnated with the same calcium compounds found in mollusk shells, though joints make them flexible, and the outermost branches are often flattened, allowing water to rush over them more easily. Some species have chunky, wide segments and others are feathery and filamentous. Despite the coralline reds' tough armor, the lined chiton and a couple types of limpets prefer them over anything else and have extra-hardened radular teeth to crunch their way through the algae.

### ENCRUSTING CORALLINE ALGAE

(up to 3/8 inch thick / low intertidal to subtidal)

There are quite a few species of encrusting coralline red algae—all look like a stony pink crust—and while there is much variety in thickness and reproductive structures, it would take an expert with a microscope to identify which one you've found. Encrusting corallines can be found on rocks, mollusk shells, and in tiny patches on blades of surfgrass. They are slow-growing but long-lived: up to fifty years.

# FLOWERING PLANTS

## SURFGRASS

(to 3 feet long / low intertidal to subtidal)

Surfgrass is not an alga: it is the only flowering plant that grows on rocks in rough ocean habitats (another type of sea grass grows in calmer water). The bright green blades are very narrow but extremely tough, and the "lawn" makes a great place for algae and other creatures to call home.

# APPENDIX

*Scientific and Common Names*

SEA ANEMONES

*Anthopleura xanthogrammica* (giant green anemone)
*Anthopleura elegantissima* (aggregating anemone)
*Anthopleura sola* (sunburst anemone)
*Corynactis californica* (strawberry anemone)
*Epiactis prolifera* (brooding anemone)
*Metridium senile* (frilled anemone)
*Tealia lofotensis* (white-spotted rose anemone)

SPONGES

*Halichondria* sp. (breadcrumb sponge)
*Haliclona* sp.
*Leucilla nuttingi* (vase sponge)
*Microciona* sp. (red sponge)

MOLLUSKS

*Aeolidia papillosa* (shag rug nudibranch)
*Anisodoris nobilis* (Pacific sea lemon)

*Chlorostoma brunnea* (brown turban snail)
*Chlorostoma funebralis* (black turban snail)
*Cryptochiton stelleri* (gumboot chiton)
*Diaulula sandiegensis* (ringed dorid)
*Diodora aspera* (keyhole limpet)
*Enteroctopus dofleini* (giant Pacific octopus)
*Haliotis rufescens* (red abalone)
*Hermissenda crassicornis* (opalescent nudibranch)
*Katharina tunicata* (black katy chiton)
*Littorina scutulata* and *L. keenae* (periwinkles)
*Lottia digitalis* (ribbed limpet)
*Lottia gigantea* (owl limpet)
*Lottia scabra* (rough limpet)
*Mopalia muscosa* (mossy chiton)
*Mytilus californianus* (California mussel)
*Nucella canaliculata* and *N. emarginata* (dog whelks)
*Rostanga pulchra* (red sponge dorid)
*Tonicella lineata* (lined chiton)
*Triopha catalinae* (sea clown nudibranch)

## WORMS

*Harmothoe imbricata* (scale worm)
*Nereis* sp. (clam worm)
*Phascolosoma agassizi* (peanut worm)
*Phragmatopoma californica* (honeycomb tube worm)
*Serpula* sp. (plume worm)
*Spirorbis* sp. (spirorbid worm)

## ARTHROPODS

*Balanus glandula* (acorn barnacle)
*Cancer productus* (red rock crab)

*Hemigrapsus nudus* (purple shore crab)
*Hemigrapsus oregonensis* (green shore crab)
*Idotea* sp. (isopod)
*Metacarcinus magister* (Dungeness crab)
*Pachygrapsus crassipes* (lined shore crab)
*Pagurus hirsutiusculus* and *P. samuelis* (hermit crabs)
*Petrolisthes eriomerus* (porcelain crab)
*Pollicipes polymerus* (gooseneck barnacle)
*Pugettia producta* (kelp crab)
*Pycnogonum* sp. (sea spider)
*Romaleon antennarium* (Pacific rock crab)

ECHINODERMS
*Dermasterias imbricata* (leather star)
*Henricia leviuscula* (blood star)
*Leptasterias* sp. (six-rayed star)
*Ophiothrix spiculata* (brittle star)
*Patiria miniata* (bat star)
*Pisaster ochraceus* (ochre sea star)
*Pycnopodia helianthoides* (sunflower star)
*Strongylocentrotus purpuratus* (purple sea urchin)

TUNICATES
*Aplidium californicum* (sea pork)
*Archidistoma psammion* (sandy slab sea squirt)
*Clavelina huntsmani* (light bulb tunicate)
*Distaplia occidentalis* (mushroom ascidian)
*Styela montereyensis* (stalked tunicate)

## FISHES

*Apodichthys fucorum* (rockweed gunnel)
*Cebidichthys violaceus* (monkeyface prickleback)
*Oligocottus maculosus* (tide pool sculpin)
*Xiphister mucosus* (rock prickleback)

## BIRDS

*Arenaria melanocephala* (Black Turnstone)
*Haematopus bachmani* (Black Oystercatcher)
*Larus* sp. (gull)

## MARINE ALGAE

*Cladophora columbiana* (pin cushion algae)
*Corallina* sp. (upright coralline algae)
*Corallina* sp. (encrusting coralline algae)
*Egregia menziesii* (feather boa kelp)
*Fucus distichus* (rockweed)
*Iridaea flaccida* (iridescent algae)
*Laminaria setchellii* (laminaria)
*Macrocystis pyrifera* (giant kelp)
*Mastocarpus papillatus* (Turkish washcloth)
*Mazzaella affinis* (Turkish towel)
*Nereocystis luetkeana* (bull kelp)
*Pelvetia* sp. (slender rockweed)
*Phyllospadix* sp. (surfgrass)
*Porphyra* sp. (purple laver)
*Postelsia palmaeformis* (sea palm)
*Ulva* sp. (sea lettuce)

# REFERENCES

Buchsbaum, Ralph. *Animals without Backbones.* Chicago: Univ. of Chicago Press, 1962.

Davenport, Julia Copple. *Sanctuary Explorations.* Santa Cruz, CA: Univ. of California, Santa Cruz, Institute of Marine Sciences, Joseph M. Long Marine Lab, 1997.

Dawson, E. Yale, and Michael S. Foster. *Seashore Plants of California.* Berkeley: Univ. of California Press, 1982.

Gunzi, Christiane. *Tide Pool.* New York: DK Publishing, 1998.

Hedgpeth, Joel W. *Introduction to Seashore Life of the San Francisco Bay Region and the Coast of Northern California.* Berkeley: Univ. of California Press, 1967.

Hedgpeth, Joel W., Edward F. Ricketts, and Jack Calvin. *Between Pacific Tides.* 4th ed. Stanford, CA: Stanford, Univ. Press, 1968.

Morris, Robert Harding, Donald P. Abbott, and Eugene C. Haderlie. *Intertidal Invertebrates of California.* Stanford, CA: Stanford Univ. Press, 1980.

Moyle, Peter B. *Fish: An Enthusiast's Guide.* Berkeley: Univ. of California Press, 1995.

National Geographic Society. *Field Guide to the Birds of North America.* 2d ed. Washington, DC: National Geographic Society, 1987.

Niesen, Thomas M. *The Marine Biology Coloring Book.* New York: HarperCollins (Coloring Concepts, Inc.), 1982

Rosenfeld, Anne Wertheim, and Robert T. Paine. *The Intertidal Wilderness.* Berkeley: Univ. of California Press, 2002.

## INTERNET RESOURCES

Animal Diversity Web, animaldiversity.ummz.umich.edu

Burdick, Alan. "The Chemistry of... Glue", Discover (Feb. 2003), www.discovermagazine.com/2003/feb/featchem

CalPhotos, calphotos.berkeley.edu

Dental Tribune International, www.dental-tribune.com

Edmonds Discovery Programs, www.edmondswa.gov/services/education/discovery-programs

Encyclopedia of Life, eol.org

Exploring Rocky Shores of Southern Oregon Coast, www.oregontidepooling.com

iNaturalist, www.inaturalist.org

Intertidal Invertebrates of the Monterey Bay Area, California, people.ucsc.edu/~mcduck/DreamWeaver

Lafskey, Melissa. "Worm Glue May Hold the Key to Fixing Broken Bones." Discovery, Discoblog (Nov. 25, 2008), http://blogs.discovermagazine.com/discoblog/2008/11/25

LiMPETS (Rocky Intertidal Monitoring), www.limpetsmonitoring.org/rocky-intertidal-monitoring

"Nucella lapillus," BIOTIC (Biological Traits Information Catalogue), www.marlin.ac.uk/biotic/browse.php?sp=4288

Scholastic, http://teacher.scholastic.com/researchtools/researchstarters/oceans/index.htm

ScienceBlogs,www.scienceblogs.com/

SeaNet (Common Marine Organisms of Monterey Bay, California), seanet.stanford.edu

Seaweed Industry Association, seaweedindustry.com

The Seaweed Site, www.seaweed.ie

Shorelines (Smithsonian Environmental Research Center), sercblog.si.edu

SIMoN (Sanctuary Integrated Monitoring Network), www.sanctuarysimon.org

A Snail's Odyssey, asnailsoddyssey.com

Tree of Life Web Project, www.tolweb.org

An Underwater Field Guide to Pt Lobos, www.pt-lobos.com

University of California Museum of Paleontology, www.ucmp.berkeley.edu

University of Puget Sound, www.pugetsound.edu.academics/academic-resources/slater-museum/exhibits/marine-panel

Walla Walla University (Rosario Beach Marine Laboratory), www.wallawalla. edu

Washington State University Beach Watchers, www.beachwatchers.wsu.edu

# ABOUT THE AUTHOR

MARNI FYLLING FELL IN LOVE with marine invertebrates the first time she looked through a dissecting scope in zoology lab at UC Davis. This inspired her to take a field marine invertebrate biology class at the Bodega Marine Lab, and she's never looked back. A science illustrator, writer, and educator, her favorite thing to do is explore tide pools, although sketching insects and wildflowers (or just about anything else) is a close second.

*Photo courtesy of Rowan Ellison*